W9-BIE-813

PASSION FOR PILGRIMAGE

PASSION
FOR PILGRIMAGE

Notes for the Journey Home

MEDITATIONS ON THE EASTER MYSTERY

ALAN JONES

MOREHOUSE PUBLISHING

Copyright © 1989 by Alan Jones

Published in 1999 by
Morehouse Publishing
P.O. Box 1321
Harrisburg, PA 17105

Morehouse Publishing is a division of The Morehouse Group.

All rights reserved. No part of this book may be reproduced or transmitted in any form or by any means, electronic or mechanical, including photocopying, recording, or by any information storage and retrieval system, without written permission from the publisher.

Printed in the United States of America

Study Questions by Helen C. L. McPeak, an Episcopal priest in Northern California

Cover design by Corey Kent

Excerpts on pages 91, 115, and 124 are from *W. H. Auden: Collected Poems* by W.H. Auden, edited by Edward Mendelson. Copyright © 1944 and renewed 1972 W. H. Auden. Reprinted by permission of Random House, Inc.

Excerpt on pages 159–160 is from "Shadows" from *The Complete Poems of D. H. Lawrence*, by D. H. Lawrence, edited by V. de Sola Pinto & F. W. Roberts. Copyright © 1964, 1971 by Angelo Ravagli and C. M. Weekley, Executors of the Estate of Frieda Lawrence Ravagli. Used by permission of Viking Penguin, a division of Penguin Putnam Inc.

Library of Congress Cataloging—in—Publication Data

Jones, Alan W., 1940–
    Passion for pilgrimage : notes for the journey home : meditations on the Easter mystery / Alan Jones.
        p.   cm.
    Originally published: San Francisco : Harper & Row, c1989.
    Includes bibliographical references.
    ISBN 0-8192-1823-5 (pbk. : alk. paper)
    1. Lent Meditations. 2. Easter Meditations. I. Title.
BV85.J62   1999
242' .34—dc21   99-32673
                                                              CIP

For the Community of Grace Cathedral,
San Francisco

With love and admiration

"When the time comes for me to gather you,
I will bring you home."—*Zephaniah 3:20*

(From the Great Vigil of Easter)

CONTENTS

PREFACE

The Christian faith came as the result of the collision of two passions: God's Passion for us and our passion for God. I have written this book after several years of preaching and teaching the Passion and of trying to preach and teach it passionately. Year by year we tell the story, and year by year I have tried to "get it right!" But it is impossible to catch the spirit of a love affair in mere words. The only thing to do is to go on telling the story in as many different ways as possible in the hope that some new variation may awaken another human being and set him or her on pilgrimage.

The preacher and teacher seeks to be an instrument of the Spirit who aches to transform our drifting into pilgrimage. In spite of the fact that it is the same old story, it bears repeating over and over again. In the end, the story becomes something we find ourselves actually living rather than merely hearing. In fact, the story is not so much something that we live as something that lives us. But do we know the story that speaks to our hurts, hopes, and longings? Here's what happened. Jesus Christ (one of *us*) took a journey through growing, suffering, and loving. The story of his death and Resurrection is a great gift to those who allow it to connect with the depths of their own aching. The simple fact is that the Story of Jesus is also *our* story. It is the means by which we can go through life with meaning and hope.

These meditations are attempts to tell "the same old story." They weave a repetitive pattern around the themes of passion, pilgrimage, and our longing for "home." In fact, they can be summed up in the phrase, *Come home! All is forgiven!*

It is impossible to write on such themes without acknowledging one's passionate connection with the human community, with people who believe and who want to believe. Then there is the closer circle of connection: friends who go on loving and caring when I wander far from "home." Gratitude is a natural response to such kindness. Three people deserve special mention: the Right

Reverend William Swing, bishop of California, friend and mentor, who has taught me how to be more at home in that strangest of institutions, the Christian Church; the Very Reverend Alan Webster, former dean of St. Paul's Cathedral, London, who has, for some twenty years, been a good companion on the road home; and my wife, Josephine, who has taught me much about how we are already "at home" even when on pilgrimage.

Alan Jones
Grace Cathedral
San Francisco

Introduction:
Broken Bones May Joy!

The Church's Year celebrates and gives us the opportunity to deepen our wildest longings. Nothing need be left out. The cycle includes bad times as well as good. There is wounding and healing, dying and rising. We celebrate new beginnings, and we give due honor to times for dying. This rhythm of dying and rising, of fasting and feasting, corresponds to something deep within us. The latter provides occasions for rejoicing; the former helps us clarify exactly what it is we are celebrating. Allan Bloom describes the reason behind Plato's *Symposium* (dinner conversation) as an opportunity for friends to come together and tell wonderful stories about the meaning of their longing.[1] This is also a good description of the round of stories we tell, over and over again, in the Church's Year. It is especially true of that season of the year known as Lent. We tell and retell the story of the great Passion: God's longing for us and our longing for God. The stories are maps for a journey back to God and to ourselves. This book is a tribute to the wonderful story of God's Passion and love for us, which speak to our deepest longings.

We live, however, in a time when the stories of our longing are being forgotten. They still have the power to move us, but we don't know how to allow them to change us, to heal us, to give us new life. For example, the musical version of Victor Hugo's masterpiece *Les Miserables* enjoyed great commercial success on both the London and New York stages. It is a wonderful story about the meaning of our longing. It speaks to our ache for reconciliation and resurrection. In fact, it is deeply Christian. When my family and I saw it, people were in tears, and there was a standing ovation. But I couldn't help wonder how many of the audience recognized the story's origins and connected it with what goes on in our churches Sunday by Sunday. There is no sense of blame in this, although there is a feeling of regret that the churches don't tell the story in such a way that it connects with our longing. It may be that regular church people are too close to the story and, in taking it for granted, miss its wonder and glory. Nevertheless, I know of no other place where the story is told over and over again with passion and conviction.

Twenty years ago, an old friend of mine wrote a book about reconciliation and resurrection called *Broken Bones May Joy.*[2] The title was taken from a poem by the sixteenth-century poet and country parson George Herbert. The words sound a little strange to our ears, but they convey, in six short lines, the whole Christian witness to human longing.

> *But thou wilt sin and grief destroy;*
> *That so the broken bones may joy,*
> *And tuned together in a well-set song*
> *Full of his praises*
> *Who dead men raises*
> *Fractures well cured make us more strong.*

I mention my friend and his use of George Herbert because my own experience of resurrection has been through the gracious agency of other storytellers. My brokenness has known healing because others have reached out to touch. Not only are the living my friends, but so also are the dead: those who have "died in the Lord," and "those whose faith is known to God alone." The Story of Christianity is about the mending of the world so that broken bones may rejoice. Christianity is a passion for reconciliation and resurrection. It is the story of a pilgrimage, passionately undertaken for the sake of love. Ours is a pilgrimage towards wholeness in companionship with every human being. Father Zossima, in Dostoyevski's *Brothers Karamazov*, insists, "Everyone of us has sinned against all, and, therefore, everyone is responsible for all to all for everything." Is this a great truth or a great and even harmful nonsense? It is a great truth that speaks directly to our longing and our dread. Such an overwhelming sense of solidarity with all human beings and the call to an all-embracing pilgrimage are bound to force us to encounter brokenness in every aspect of human life, from our most intimate relations to the world of international politics. How would we go about applying Father Zossima's maxim to Archbishop Tutu's South Africa or to the issues of human passions focused on AIDS, abortion, or nuclear disarmament? Lent, therefore is not only a healing time when "broken bones may joy." It is also a time for the asking of hard questions and the facing of hard choices. I have to face up to the choice between good and evil and admit my own complicity in the evils of the world. I am convinced that such probing is part of the honest work of love. It is an experience of passion. It is that which drives me to my knees. The more we are able to face our own capacity for evil the less likely we are to spread the disease. That is why a period of discipline such as Lent can be a stretching and exciting time. It challenges us to confront the deep mystery of those who repel and disgust us. It is an opportunity for us to gain a fresh understanding of ourselves and our world.

Lent is, therefore, a time of bringing order out of our chaos. Its disciplines are for the sake of our learning the Love Story over again, so that it becomes second nature to us. We should, however, never underestimate our unwillingness to embrace new insights, especially if those insights push us into pilgrimage and thereby challenge our patterns of behavior and threaten our settled way of life. Better to see *Les Miserables*, feel moved (but not too much), buy a T-shirt, and go back to "business as usual." The Lenten Passion Story, with its attendant challenge to disciplined attention, is about our longing for freedom and our fear of it. It challenges me to look at my "addictions" and look at those parts of me that I dread the most—my weaknesses and my failures. The Passion Story cannot connect with those who are addicted to being in control or who have addled themselves with the passion for power or security. This Passion Story is for those who are, to some degree, in touch with their longing.

Christian discipline places us in a situation of vulnerability by bringing us to the end or our rope. Its purpose is to show that, in the end, our efforts don't work! From time to time I need to be made to feel the extent of my helplessness, so that I can say, with complete candor, "I can't cope. This is really beyond me." It is at that moment of admission that some new and good begins to happen to me. I begin to live from a center other than my self-protecting, manipulating ego. I begin to *move* in a new direction. My drifting is consecrated into pilgrimage. I begin to live with my longing. Far from finding myself on a masochistic, psychological "trip," a minor miracle occurs. I am sufficiently "out of the way" for a while that I get a glimpse of what it might mean to love without strings.

The Church has a special name for this process of discovery. It's called repentance. Repentance is the way we make a new beginning. That is why I "go to confession" regularly: to acknowledge my weakness and to celebrate the possibility of new beginnings. The sacrament of reconciliation helps me find and identify my longing and sets me on the road to the freedom for which I ache and from which I sometimes turn in dread. Freedom brings with it the terrible burden of responsibility. That is why we dread it. Freedom is also the prerequisite for any kind of genuine loving. That is why we long for it. I respect my dread of hard choices. But love eludes me until I begin to make them. When I refuse to pay attention to my longing, I get lost, and broken bones are not healed.

Lent then is a unique opportunity to retell the story of God's Passion for us in the context of hope. When we are truly brought to the end of our rope, we find that God's "yoke is easy and burden light." We find that we can extend our horizons and welcome a wider variety of our brothers and sisters into the circle of our loving. God's will is that, when we finally reach our destination, no one will be left out. Charles Peguy wrote that, when we reach heaven at the end of our pilgrimage, God will ask this searching question: "Où sont les austres!" Where are the others? The Easter promise of new life is for everyone. In this homecoming, everyone is included.

We cannot, however, leave the question of our longing there, at the gates of heaven. We are given a glimpse, now and then, of the end of our journeying, but we aren't there yet. The brokenness of the world keeps breaking in. If we are to be agents of reconciliation and resurrection in the world, we have to take a long hard look at our own sinning. The trouble is we have been brought up in a society that finds it unusually painful to admit moral failure. As one commentator puts it:

> As every schoolchild learns before he or she reaches the age of ten, America is always and forever innocent. Foreigners commit crimes against humanity. Americans make well-intentioned mistakes. Foreigners incite wars, embrace communism, sponsor terrorists, and smuggle cocaine into Connecticut. Americans cleanse the world of its impurities.
>
> True, a few hundred thousand peasants might come to grief in Southeast Asia because of an American mistake. True, American corporations enhance the yields of their industry with their talent for price-fixing, theft, loan-sharking, and fraud. But their crimes, being American, can be understood as temporary breakdowns in the otherwise flawless machinery of the American soul. The fault is never one of character or motive. Americans receive their virtue from heaven, as part of their inheritance and proof of their natural aptitude for goodness.[3]

Our country suffers from the twin agonies of imagined perfection on the one hand and nagging self-doubt on the other. What is worse, according to this jaundiced view of the state of the American soul, is that we live in an "illusion of grace." That is our glory and our tragedy. There's glory in our trust that we are a peculiar and graced people, tragedy because our belief in our election is largely an illusion. The question is how do we move out of "an illusion of grace" into the real thing? The old answer from religion, as we have seen, is "Repent!" Lent begins with a call to repentance. The way out of illusion and into the place of newness and healing is through a change of heart, a willingness to slough off old habits.

Repentance, in today's terms, requires three simple commitments: the first is to rigorous honesty—that is, to hope for nothing less than the truth. The second is to honor our passion for connection by celebrating the solidarity of all human beings. The third is to search for a common language, so that we can talk to each other. This is what repentance means. We are to tell the truth, love each other, and form a Commonwealth—all of which require a *common* language. This is our agenda. All three will bring us closer to understanding the meaning of our longing.

First, repentance, understood as a commitment to a rigorous honesty, involves serious changes in our lives. Our clinging to a virtuous view of ourselves is our greatest vice, and we have developed it into a fine art. Lies not only block the possibility of new life promised by a change of heart but also take a great deal of energy to maintain. Repentance isn't a matter of beating our breasts and saying that deep down we're rotten. Repentance is hoping for nothing less than the truth. If we don't, we lose touch with our deepest selves, with each other and with God. Repentance—hoping for and trusting in nothing less than the truth—also means paying attention to our passion for connection. Our passion for connection is a passion for heaven. The lure of disconnection is the lure of hell. And both energies are at work in America today.

Second, repentance requires that we honor our passion for connection. We long for it, and yet we are terrified of it. "Only connect," the novelist, E. M. Forster, tells us. "Only we can't!" is the response. We have become allied to disconnection in the name of keeping our souls pure. "Purity" requires that we disassociate ourselves from all sorts of classes of people and limit our view of the Commonwealth. We exclude the unworthy, the unattractive, and the morally impure from our perfect state. We "live" by strategies of exclusion and disconnection. Religion is one of the weapons by which we keep our distance from each other.

Third, repentance involves our recovering a common language. Consider for a moment the range of people who call themselves Christians. We hold differing religious convictions. Some have rejected formal religion altogether. What could possibly unite us—bind us together in a creative way? I mean what *positive* thing? There are plenty of negative energies that bind us together. Common enemies (real or imagined) and the bread-and-circuses mentality of popular politics provide the glue of temporary connection. Sentimentality sometimes unites us. A haze of goodwill, which refuses to face real differences, can keep us going for a while. But nothing seems to last. The road to repentance involves a commitment to truth wherever it may lead, and therefore, a true passion for connection requires not the blurring of distinctions but their acknowledgement. In order to repent we need a common language and place to meet. But our language is polluted, and nowhere is it more polluted than in the realms of politics and religion.

The search for Civic or Moral Community leads us to a truthful acknowledgment of the depths of our bankruptcy and spiritual poverty. We have come to the end of our rope. We are beginning to suffer from the debilitating impact of our assuming that our individualism and pluralism are God's gifts to us. There isn't much holding us together. Repentance, a change of heart—a change of habits—is a call to return to truth-telling and love-making by celebrating our solidarity with one another. Language is important for our return. Telling the Story of God's Passion for us helps to bring us home.

The theme is an ancient one. Human beings are always losing their way. We lost ours when we began taking ideological pluralism and political liberalism for granted—as if to say, "These truths we hold to be self-evident." Individualism has lead us into private worlds of selective connections. Pluralism has introduced us to ways in which we can live comfortably with collective irresponsibility in the name of freedom. We have ended up nowhere with nothing to say to each other. There is no place for us to tell wonderful stories about the meaning of our longing. The Church, for all its faults, guards the memory and provides the *place*.

Some of the attempts to find our way back scare me to death. There are extremist, paramilitary, fascist "Christian" groups. The routine rhetoric of the Far Right and Far Left offer no real hope. We need to articulate common values and meanings if we are to survive and flourish. In intellectual terms, we need to recover an underlying "conceptual architecture" so that we can *talk* to each other. If we don't, we will inhabit smaller and smaller private worlds. All that will be left of civil discourse will be the inane exchange of slogans and the trading of anathemas. As one critic has asked, "…is our vaunted pluralism naught but an uneasy compromise, which threatens at any moment to disintegrate into a triumph of fundamentalist intolerance or secularist anti-religion?"[4]

What a choice! I, for one, do not want to choose between the two emerging *establishments* of pan-Protestant evangelicalism, on the one hand, and an aggressive anti-religious secular culture, on the other. A plague on both their houses! If either showed any signs of self-criticism I would be happier, but as it is, I have no place to join in even to argue. There is no place to meet and talk. There's no place for me to share my longings, so that I might understand them better. That is why the annual opportunity for storytelling that Lent offers is so important. It is a special time when our passion for connection is honored, not by bland and banal rituals, but by the telling of a tough and passionate story.

The problem is that our society is, to use old-fashioned categories, polytheistic and neopagan. These serve definite political ends. The authorities of the Roman Empire encouraged polytheism. Private gods for personal use are politically very handy. We can play one god off against another. That is why the Jews were distrusted, hated, and persecuted. Their ardent monotheism and their passion for a unified moral order made them potential enemies of the state. In our day "our fanatical pluralism [undercuts] the vitality, as well as the moral and cultural influence, of religion in the world, and [leaves] the field to the kind of techno-political Caesarism of the twentieth century."[5] Our polytheism (which is a code word for our cancerous individualism and irresponsible pluralism) simply cannot provide the unitive framework we need. We long for a common story. We ache for *shared* meanings. We see the intellectual bankruptcy of "polytheism" in our own political system. Politicians encourage it for their own ends, even claiming to be "born again" (but with no Church allegiance, of course) if it suits their purpose.

Our commitment to an uncritical pluralism forces us to surrender our intelligence in a sort of intellectual equivalent of alcoholism.

We think, for example, that we must have an uncritical respect for people's religious beliefs, no matter how bizarre and barbarous. We are tempted to glorify the neurotic and the pathological in the name of diversity. What was Jonestown if not an aberration? Is every crazy cult merely an instance of the "varieties of religious experience"? The truth is that the relativizing binge we've been on for the past twenty years is coming to an end. It is time to get off the booze and sober up. We need to break out of our addictive little worlds: those "privatized, syncretistic, psycho-spiritual" experiments of middle-class consumer society.[6] We are so busy fulfilling ourselves, pursuing happiness, that we miss each other. We don't take the time to tell each other the stories that reveal our longing. There is no meeting, no real confrontation, no genuine engagement. No living *word* connects us. *The* word to reforge connection is repentance.

Repentance—a change of heart—unleashes not only passion for connection but also a desire for justice. But unless we can *talk* to each other, justice eludes us—a sure sign of the apocalyptic nature of the times. As one critic has observed, "The barbarians are not waiting beyond the frontiers; they have already been governing us for some time."[7] Barbarous times require strategies for pilgrims.

The Bible is a handbook for pilgrims. It is a repository of wonderful stories. The three ingredients of repentance are there: the commitment to honesty, the passion for connection, and the healing power of a common language. In Lent we rehearse the Story of God's Passion, which offers us some powerful images with regard to our passion for and our fear of connection. The Bible provides us with unifying images of great moral energy that liberate us from the tiny lifestyle enclaves that enslave us. It invites us into a world of common memories that form the basis for our experiencing ourselves as *one* people. That is where the fundamentalists are right. They see, with great clarity, the necessity of a common life based on shared experience.

Since our capacity for self-deception is almost infinite, we need, from time to time, a hammer blow of prophetic truth to wake us up to the real situation. The prophets tell us the times are desperate, we've lost our way, we are disconnected from God and from each other, and it's time to come home. That is why religion cannot be relegated to a private world. Its message is public. It is to be proclaimed from the housetops.

In Malachi, chapters 3 and 4, for example, the prophet laments the continuing "bad faith" of the people. He knows that struggle for values and meaning is hard work. The miracle of meaning often comes only after a dark night of faithful waiting. The things that matter require constant vigilance for their maintenance. The people whom Malachi addresses are spiritually lazy and morally exhausted. They take a short-term view of everything. And why not? The arrogant are blessed, and evildoers make a good living. Such a view of the world, however, is a sure sign of a dulled sensibility. The people cannot discriminate between good and evil. The soul becomes coarse and gross. The return to God requires our being able to see clearly so that we can tell the good from the bad, the true from the false. The prophet warns the people that the Day will come "burning like an oven" when the arrogant and evil will be consumed like stubble, all of them "root and branch." God will send Elijah before the great and terrible Day of the Lord. That Day will surely come. The question is, is it something to look forward to? It seems as if "the wonderful stories" of our longing are, in reality, tales of doom.

These mighty, biblical stories were taken for granted by John Winthrop, preaching to the crew and passengers on the *Arabella* anchored in Massachusetts Bay in 1630. The only way to avoid the "shipwracke" of God's wrath in this great venture

> *is to follow the counsell of Michah, to doe justly, to love mercy, to walk humbly with our God. For this end, wee must be knitt together in this worke as one man, we must entertaine each other in brotherly Affeccion, we much be willing to abridge ourselves of our superfluities, for the supply of others necessities, we must uphold a familiar Commerce together in all meekness, gentleness and patience and liberality. Wee must delight in each other, make others Condicions our own, rejoyce together, mourne together, labour and suffer together, always*

*having before our eyes our Commission and Community in
the work, our Community as members of the same body, soe
shall we keep the unity of the spirit in the bond of peace.*

The Bible is the stuff of which our history, both individually
and as a people, is made. We can begin to recover the
Commonwealth by learning to welcome truth, from whatever
quarter, with a passion. There *are* things on which we *do* agree. We
may want to argue and argue passionately about their meaning.
Any talking together about anything that matters is sure to involve
argument and disagreement. We seek to enlarge the boundaries of
the conversation to include everyone, especially those who have no
voice—so that broken bones may joy.

The Commonwealth of God includes everyone. Passion for that
Commonwealth is focused on the table around which Christians
gather Sunday by Sunday. The table is open to all. There is enough
for everyone. This is Christianity's peculiar way of saying what other
traditions proclaim in other ways. *Together* we decry the fact that
"the hungry and the homeless people in this nation are no part of
anything worthy of being called a commonwealth. The extent of
their suffering shows how far we are from being a community of
persons."[8] The extent of our passion for honesty and connection will
determine what kind of society we will inhabit and whether that
society will bear the marks of heaven or hell.

We begin our pilgrimage with a call to repentance. Repent and
return to the Lord! There is one table, one Commonwealth. In this,
we are, with all the people of the earth, *graced.* The life of grace,
however, rests on neither a natural aptitude for goodness, nor of
the imagined flawless machinery of the American soul. The life of
grace rests on our willingness to place ourselves "under the mercy"
(as the old phrase has it). The mercy of God enables us to abridge
ourselves of our superfluities, delight in each other, rejoice *together*,
mourn *together*, labor and suffer *together*. There is not one of us who
is not "well connected," joined as we are in one communion and fellowship in God's Commonwealth. The Church is the sacrament of
this Commonwealth, which is a community of all for all. The

Church is the place where the wonderful story that will make us into one People is told over and over again. It is a Love Story about the mending of broken bones; it is a Passion Story about the joy of homecoming.

STUDY QUESTIONS

1. Why "pilgrimage?" What leads you to read a book about this particular topic? What hopes and expectations do you have of this study?

2. Jones writes of our living in a time when the stories of our longings have been forgotten. How well have you come to know and live the Christian story? Who was instrumental in your learning it?

3. Repentance, Jones says, is a process of discovering that, in the end, our efforts don't work. He suggests three simple commitments required by the change of heart that is repentance. Review these three commitments (p. 6). Which of these hold particular challenge for you? For your community? Look up "repentance" in the dictionary.

4. Jones warns us never to "underestimate our unwillingness to embrace new insights" (p. 3). He says that our capacity for self-deception is almost infinite, demanding "a hammer blow of prophetic truth to wake us up" (p. 9). What resources does Jones offer for maintaining our corporate awareness of the Passion Story?

I.
THE LENTEN JOURNEY

1.
THE SAME OLD STORY

We are actors in a Passion Story about the joy of homecoming. We may, however, be tempted to give up the dramatic project we call our life before we even begin. After all, isn't it the same old story, the same old folly, we the same tragic ending? I am often overcome by the thought that my years are running out and I seem to play the same old tune. I wonder if anything really new can happen to me. Even if we have only a vague sense of history we can see how pointless it all is. Life is "a tale told by an idiot, full of sound and fury and signifying nothing." This is a cry of a despairing man caught up in the drama not of his own choosing. Are we not similarly caught up in an inexorable drama, with no guarantee of a joyful homecoming? Some seem to find their way through to a kind of happiness but isn't that at the expense of seeing the whole picture? If it's the same old story, where is the promise of freedom? Is it possible that the telling of the old, old story is a way of opening us up to new possibilities? The season of Lent involves the telling of the same old story that invites us to become participants in the drama. If we choose to act in this great Passion Play we shall find ourselves called to be experiments in vulnerability. We will have set in motion a course of events totally beyond our control.

Not long ago, just as the season of Lent has got underway, a friend complained to me, "I know it's Lent, but where's the joy?" It is easy to understand why Lent is often misunderstood as a period of savage and destructive negativity. Doesn't it encourage a despairing view of life "full of sound and fury"? It begins, after all, with Ash Wednesday and the grim reminder that we are dust and to dust we shall return. This is hardly the prelude to a party! Nevertheless, reminders of our mortality are salutary. Understood in the context of a life of faith, they prepare us for a celebration. Lent is about getting ready for a banquet, about preparing for a wild party. While there can be a great deal of fun in a spur-of-the-moment party, the preparation for a great banquet takes a lot of time and effort. Getting ourselves ready for this particular wild celebration demands our being willing to be probed by hard questions about the meaning of our longing. This particular party requires that we bring with us, especially, our passion and our need. We live in an age when everything has to be palatable and easily digestible. Hard questions and tough decisions have to be reduced to the consistency of cream of wheat. We have neither the stomach nor the teeth for solid food. Lent, however, is a time when real meat is served to feed the mind as well as the soul. There used to be a steak house in New York that displayed a sign: "If you find our steaks tough, then quit. We don't want weaklings here!" Lent is a serious time and, if the moment is right, it can present us with life and death issues. It isn't, however, meant to be a *grim* time. It is an opportunity for truth-telling, for our discovering the true grounds of joy and hope. It is often hard to strike a balance between the struggle and the joy. Perhaps that is why popular religion tends to come in two forms: the vindictive and the sentimental. The vindictive preacher threatens his hearers with hellfire, while the sentimentalist pours out a cheapened and easily digestible cream-of-wheat kind of "love." What we crave is a glimpse of the joy in the struggle, of hope *in* our pain. What we long for is to be actors in a drama with substance.

Let us begin with a question. Do you really know how to enjoy the world? Do you know how to enjoy yourself? One of the greatest parables in the New Testament has to do with the search for enjoyment and fulfillment (Luke 15:11–32). The Prodigal Son thought he knew what joy was. He had to wander far away from "home" (his true joy) to find his heart's desire. The journey home for the festivities takes us through miles of alien territory. Literature abounds with figures searching for home, for heaven. Dante goes to hell to find heaven. Faust sells his soul. Milton's Adam and Eve lose paradise. Wandering off, far from our true selves, is, paradoxically, the way back to who we truly are. There are many names for this pilgrimage to our joy. Jungian psychology, for example, calls it individuation (a very dull term for such an exciting process). There are many descriptions and stories concerning the search for joy. Underneath are questions about where "home" really is, about the way there, and about what we can expect when we arrive. In order to find our way back we have to be willing to be actors in the drama of our homecoming. An actor in a drama is given a certain character to play. He or she has to become a new person to be convincing. A great actor so embodies his or her character that we are caught up in the action and we "believe" that there, before our eyes, *is* Hamlet or the Phantom of the Opera, or St. Joan. Acting requires embodiment, incarnation, being genuinely present in the here and now. The difference between us and a real actor is that we are playing ourselves or, rather, we are searching for our true selves so that we may play our part more and more fully.

Do you really know how to be truly present, here and now? Do you know what it is not only to have a body but to *be* a body? In short, do you know how to enjoy the world? Do we really know how to enjoy each other? Are we "at home" in our bodies? We will never be able to answer these questions until we ask ourselves a more fundamental one, and that is, What kind of person am I called to be in this drama? What is my role and how do I find out my part? There are as many ways of being human as there are people. What we fail to understand is that finding out what our distinct role is in the world demands that we embrace some form of discipline. True freedom involves limitation. If, for example, a poet *chooses* to write a sonnet, he or she has chosen to write within certain limits. The poem cannot be thirteen or fifteen lines and still be a sonnet. Choice involves limitation, but within those chosen limits is the possibility of infinite variety and innovation. This simple truth is one of the most difficult for us to grasp. As with a sonnet, so with a human being. It needs emphasizing: Freedom involves choice and choice implies limitation. Human beings tend to choose contradictory roles in the drama and hurt themselves and others as the story is played out. The question remains: Do you know your part? Are you really in it? Do you want to play it to the hilt? The issue is further complicated by the fact that many of us feel trapped in playing a part in a drama in which other people have control over the casting. We find ourselves playing the same tapes over and over again. The same old story becomes a ghastly repetitive cycle of addictive "happiness," anxiety, and despair. We have to be very careful about not accepting our role from anyone less that God. God is the only one who knows our part, and while our unique role may involve the playing out of tragic elements, there is glory in it and its end is joy. In fact, while the dramatic shape is set (it *is* the same old story) we, as coauthors and coactors with God, make the play up as we go along.

The paradox is that, the more we embrace the fixed form of the Drama of Death and Resurrection, the more we experience the joyful freedom of being fully alive and fully present. This principle is as applicable to the spiritual life as it is to the making of an epic poem or the writing of a sonnet. We live in an age when most of us are frantic about "being ourselves." This is all well and good. What we don't understand is that being ourselves requires submission to a particular form or shape. This is what spiritual discipline is all about. It introduces us to the dramatic shape of human life, to its form. Within that form is the promise of liberation and unspeakable joy. Isn't it time we got ourselves in shape for our role?

We talk a great deal about "getting in shape." In fact, many of us are very concerned with our bodies. No one would quarrel with the importance of a sound diet and regular exercise. We may be overweight. We may eat junk food and avoid exercise, but at least there's the goad of guilt that we should try to do better! We know what a perfect body is supposed to look like. But what about the perfection or the wholeness of the inner life? Allan Bloom suggests that we need to recover the sense of urgency with regard to the inner drama.

Utopianism is... the fire with which we must play because it is the only way we can find out who we are. We need to criticize false understandings of Utopia, but the easy way out provided by realism is deadly. As it now stands, students have powerful images of what a perfect body is and pursue it incessantly. But deprived of literary guidance, they no longer have any image of the perfect soul, and hence do not long to have one. They do not even imagine there is such a thing.[1]

Rather than utopianism (*Utopia*, after all, means nowhere), the Drama of the Passion is the fire with which we must play, because it is the only way we can find out who we are. The literary guidance of which Bloom speaks is the same *old story* told over and over again. It is a story that truly forms the soul. The first thing it does is stimulate the imagination so that we begin to entertain the idea that we have one. But we cannot concentrate on the soul at the expense of the body.

We are spirit-enlivened flesh, and we suffer a great deal already from disembodiment. We have lost a sense of the body. That is why we cannot enjoy the world. We cannot enjoy each other. To be cut off from the body is to be deprived of a lively connection with passion. We frantically try to get back in to our bodies by taking in large quantities of food and alcohol. Sex and violence are other ways to feel connected to our bodies. We dread the dead weight of matter as much as we fear "the unbearable lightness of being" when we realize that our lives have no substance. The novelist Milan Kundera writes positively about the relation of the body with the soul. The soul needs the body's weight.

> *The heaviest of burdens crushes us, we sink beneath it, it pins us to the ground. But in the love poetry of every age, the woman longs to be weighed down by the man's body. The heaviest of burdens is therefore simultaneously an image of life's most intense fulfillment. The heavier the burden, the closer our lives come to the earth, the more real and truthful they become.*[2]

The Passion Story has to be played out in our flesh. We are to feel it in our bones as human beings rooted in the earth, fully present here and now. The actor in the Passion Play needs to cultivate a sixth sense, which is an awareness of the body. This sixth faculty is called proprioception—the sense of knowing where body is. The neurosurgeon Oliver Sacks tells of a patient whose proprioceptive faculty was destroyed. She is now disembodied. She has no way to recognize the body's "heaviness." She has no sense of its place. She says, "I feel my body is blind and deaf to itself. It has no sense of itself."

Imagine what a commitment it takes to recover a sense of the body. Such commitment is a passion. Sacks tells another story of a musician who suffered from a lesion in his visual cortex. He couldn't easily recognize things. He had no sense of objects outside himself. The way he kept in touch was by singing to himself. Any interruption to his singing made him lose his connection with things. He lost touch with his clothes, with his body. The result is that he sings all the time: eating songs, dressing songs, bathing songs. In fact, he cannot do anything unless he makes it into a song.[3] I think it is the same with us "normal" persons! We need a song to sing, a story to tell, a dance to dance so that we know where we are and who we are. But we seem to have lost the art of storytelling and dreaming. Singing bits and pieces of what we know and telling snatches of half-remembered stories are better than nothing. The more we sing and tell the old, old story the less we shall be satisfied with psychological and spiritual junk food, with false and temporary means of embodiment. Individually and collectively we feed on junk food— we hum snatches of tunes, dance a few steps, tell the fragment of a story. All this keeps us alive but barely. The Church invites us into a painful and passionate process of discovering who we are by the telling of a story. It offers us the kind of food that will make us into a true body with others. We are not brought to a sense of our bodies only individually but communally as well. *Together* we make a body. We become a body when we recover the proper sense of gravity that binds us to the earth and to each other. In order to do this we must recover the lost arts of storytelling, dancing, and singing. We need to learn to dream great dreams.

Mary Durack begins her book about the pioneering of Australia (*The Rock and the Sand*) with these words: "The people of the dream watched the people of the clock come out of the sea and strike their flagstaff firmly on the sand."[4] The clock people triumphed over the dream people. The conquered dream people of the world have much to teach us about ways in which we might "find ourselves" by telling familiar stories and singing well-known tunes. In the commonplace rhythms of our lives there lies new hope and new possibilities.

Think for a moment of the idea of theme and variation in music. Milan Kundera, in his novel *The Book of Laughter and Forgetting*, reflects on the fact that Beethoven, toward the end of his life, became fascinated with composing variations on a given theme as a means of exploring infinite musical possibilities. There are two infinities: the infinity of space and time, and "the second infinity" of inward variation. The first infinity is, of course impenetrable. We cannot fill space, and time is running out for all of us. But, just as there is *freedom* in fixed poetic *forms*, so there are infinite possibilities in playing variations on the same old tune. Beethoven concentrated on plumbing the depths of the same sixteen measures.

What Beethoven discovered in his work with variations we find when we enter the Passion Story. Our lives are given "another space, another direction." The sixteen or so measures that make up our lives are suddenly fraught with significance when we make the journey into the second infinity. This journey is no less adventurous than a trip to the moon or to the planets. The journey inward is not unlike "the physicist's descent into the wondrous innards of the atom."[5]

The Easter Cycle of Stories beginning with Lent is an opportunity to go into the "innards" of things, to understand them afresh and to find in them new space and new direction. To do this we have to learn some new skills. The journey into the second infinity requires our being able to remember the basic themes of our own lives without the benefit of editorial revision. The trick is how to remember old and painful chapters in our drama without being crushed by what we have to remember. How do we recall all the hurts and pains without being crippled by the memories? Doesn't our well-being depend on a kind of amnesia? Isn't forgetfulness better than remembering? If we refuse to remember we aren't anybody. We aren't any *body*. We aren't anywhere. How then are we to remember in hope?

The important thing to realize is that ours isn't the only drama that is going on. Besides all the petty dramas of our fellow human beings, there is the Drama of God. There is an overall theme played in the heart of God. We have to listen to that tune and share in the larger drama if we are to make sense of our own. The Book of Genesis initiates the main theme of creation. Adam (not one man or male but all people) is made from the dust of the earth and given a garden to live in. These first human beings were born in a garden. The theme of a garden will return many times as we play the tune through to the end. Two gardens (Eden and Gethsemane) are connected by our singing. Our first parents were capable of dreaming great dreams. They were given a gift too hard to bear. They were crushed by a knowledge too wonderful for them. They came to a dead end, to a barren and tuneless place.

We know what it is to have knowledge that is too hard to bear. That is why we edit our lives. That is why we lie to each other. That is why some Americans want to ban books in schools. Knowledge is dangerous. Knowledge has to be prepared for. Knowledge has to be sung and danced and made into story. The ancient tune of the first Adam (with its hidden knowledge of our once being in a beautiful garden and then being expelled from it) still plays in our bones. *We know* from the inside (even though our intellect may reject the theme of Adam's Fall as a silly myth). We are people of the clock and find it difficult to sing anymore. Our capacity to dream left us when we left the garden, although the memory remains.

Our bones "remember" many measures of the old tune. We not only know from the inside the themes of a garden and an exile, we also resonate with the hope and longing for a restoration. St. Paul writes about new possibilities in the new Adam (Rom. 5:12–21). The old, old story is given a new and revolutionary twist. We are introduced to a new and startling variation. We thought we were living a "tale told by an idiot" (a relentless cycle with no possibility for innovation), when, in fact, we are living a life capable of being filled with freedom, wonder, and glory. In short, we find ourselves in a garden of delights.

To people unwilling or too jaundiced to play, all this is fanciful talk. But those who are willing to enter the Passion Story find themselves in a place of transition between the old and the new. It is a time of temptation, a time of renewal, a time when our lives are given new space and new direction. At the very beginning of the Lenten Drama, Jesus is led by the Spirit into the wilderness to be tempted by the devil! This was a deliberate act of the Holy Spirit to stretch Jesus (the New Adam) for our sake. Our stretching will be to move from being people of the clock to being people of the dream. Our struggle will be to focus our attention on the second infinity rather than the first. Jesus is tempted to compel belief by turning stones into bread, by working wonders, or by grasping at power (Matt. 4:1–11). Such actions kill the music inside us and make us forget the story. Think of the way the human community, bound together by common stories, has been wounded by the seduction of politics, the cacophony of rabble-rousing, the jingoism of foreign policy. There is also the howling dissonance made by our indifference to one another with regard to the homeless and powerless. As people of the clock, we have no time to listen to "the still sad music of humanity." The self-serving complacency of our bloated secularism makes us tone deaf and musical cretins. We know next to nothing of a common story binding us together. We know nothing of the past and hence have little hope for the future. The result is that we know neither ourselves nor each other.

Lent plunges us into the wilderness to be tempted—or rather to acknowledge our present tuneless and storyless state. It is not accidental that what we most want to do, in times of stress, is to find someone or pay someone to listen to our story. Healing demands that it be told, but we cannot make sense of our individual stories unless we see them as part of one great Drama. When we live only by the clock and give up the call to dream, we get cut off from ourselves, from one another, and from God. There is no celebration because there is nothing to celebrate. The seeds of celebration begin to grow when we enter the Passion Story and are willing to join Jesus in the wilderness. Such a willingness stirs up in us the primordial memory of a garden and a longing to return. These memories and longings are a far cry from wishful thinking and an indulgent sinking into nostalgia. Once acknowledged and fed, they become the instruments of transformation, not only of individuals, but of communities and nations as well. Such people, sometimes in gentleness, sometimes in rage, but always in faith, insist that the garden is the true reality. They are the ones who founded hospitals, schools, and universities, who fought against slavery and oppression and died as martyrs. They knew they weren't yet at home. They knew they were actors in a drama far bigger than themselves. They were possessed of a dream and, as such, were frightening to us. They burned with passion, and we also secretly longed for a passion equal to theirs. Lent creates the space for us to dare a little in the direction of passion. We begin by daring to hope for a homecoming. We already know scraps of the tune. It is now a matter of listening to the same old story to catch all of it.

As we have seen, there is one scene in the Passion Play that focuses our attention on homecoming. The Prodigal Son comes to himself—that is, he repents. The father's love frees him to forgive himself so that he may eat and be made into someone new. The narrative of the Prodigal Son is part of the same old story that carries within it the promise of genuine newness and variation. St. Paul affirms, "If any one is in Christ, he is a new creation; the old has passed away, behold the new has come" (2 Cor. 5:17, RSV). When newness breaks out in us we experience it as a passion, a kind of suffering. The newness of God breaking in on us means making room for a party, space for a banquet. It also means being in touch with the painful mystery of our own emptiness, or "lightness of being." The emptiness inside us is transformed by the Passion Story into a place of celebration, an occasion of eating and drinking. There is joy in discovering the meaning of those empty spaces within us. In developing our sixth sense, we will not only know where the body is but will realize that we are being formed into one body, by a process of story-telling, singing, and dancing. We discover that we are in this *together*. The invitation is, Let us be a body—together! Such a gathering of all humankind for a banquet is bound to involve struggle and pain. There is no way round the issue of passion. But what a party!

STUDY QUESTIONS

1. Review the key points in the Passion Story. Which elements of this drama have taken on new energy for you over time? Which seem to remain the same old story? Where do you insert yourself into this story?

2. Jones asks, "Do you really know how to enjoy the world?" (p. 16) How do you respond? In what situations are you able to be remembered, to be a body, truly present, here and now? In what situations are you unable to find connection?

3. "The church invites us into a painful and passionate process of discovering who we are by the telling of a story" (p. 20). What role or roles do you play in this process? How much of your role is shaped by your own careful preparation and hard questioning? How much is shaped by others' expectations of you? How much is imagination inspired by God? In what ways do you discern among these influences?

4. Jones writes, "Choice involves limitation, but within those chosen limits is the possibility of infinite variety and innovation" (p. 17). He also writes of the two infinities: one of time and space, which remains impenetrable, and a second of inward variation where possibilities abound (p. 21). In what ways do you find "the same old story" of the Passion limiting, and in what ways infinite? Where are the infinite possibilities of your own life?

5. "Knowledge is dangerous. Knowledge has to be prepared for. Knowledge has to be sung and danced and made into story." (p. 22). Do Jones' words seem fanciful talk? Do they draw you to a place of transition? How do you handle knowledge in your own life?

2.
THE ROAD THAT LEADS NOWHERE

How do we find our way to the party? I am puzzled why we have to get lost in order to find the road home. Falling into error seems to be a very important event on the journey. And this "falling" happens more than once. We proceed by trial and error. As we have seen, if we want to find out who and where we are, we must be willing to play with fire. John Bunyan's *Pilgrim's Progress* chronicles adventures with friends and enemies, with dead ends and obstacles. We should expect no less on our pilgrimage. The unpalatable truth is that it is possible to get lost. Perdition (which is lostness) is open to us. Our choices matter. Our behavior has consequences—even dire ones.

We cannot behave anyhow and expect to arrive at our chosen destination. We live, however, in a strange make-believe society in which people get upset because their choices have consequences! The idea that choices aren't costly is a road that leads nowhere. A difficult choice used to mean the mature accepting of "difficult consequences in the form of suffering, disapproval, punishment and guilt." Unless the consequences of choice were accepted the choice was thought to have no significance. Allan Bloom writes:

> *Accepting the consequences for affirming what really counts is what gives Antigone her nobility... Now, when we speak of the right to choice, we mean that there are no necessary consequences, that disapproval is only prejudice and guilt only a neurosis. Political activism and psychiatry can handle it... America has no-fault automobile accidents, no-fault divorces, and it is moving with the aid of modern philosophy toward no-fault choices.*[1]

We are truly nowhere without the pain and promise of lively choices. Our smallest actions and decisions can be fraught with significance and can have serious consequences. We get lost spiritually precisely in proportion to the casualness of our choices. We used to make fun of the Victorians for their supposed repressive and hypocritical view of sex. We might now and then suffer from a twinge of envy when we weigh our lightness against their heaviness.

> Great sex on a Victorian sofa is far more awkward than sex atop a Sealy posturepedic, king-size mattress, but... those violently contorted Victorian lovers will know by their cracked skulls and bumped shins that what they have engaged in is something and not nothing; hard not soft; risky not safe; productive of long and dire consequences, not immediately dismissed in a cloud of smoke from a cigarette ironically named "True."[2]

The Victorians knew that sex was about *something* and not nothing. They knew that there was no such thing as "safe sex." Safe sex is an extraordinary fantasy of our culture. Sex is never safe. It is risky and "productive of long and dire consequences." And if our sexual activity is about *something* and not just nothing, imagine what the whole of our life might be about.

Lent is a time to dig deep, deep within ourselves into the pit of self-knowledge, to examine our choices and their consequences. When we find that our choices have led us to a dead end, when it finally dawns on us that we are on a road that leads nowhere, we are in a unique place to make yet another choice—a genuinely liberating one. Choice is always a liberating possibility for us no matter how lost we are. The liberating choice I have in mind has to do with the free admission of guilt. We would rather, however, be enslaved to the myth of a guilt-free life than admit our sinfulness and be truly free. Americans like to think of themselves as innocent. There is no admission of soul sickness. How could there be in an unfallen world? This is our fantasy.

There is an indescribable liberation for the person who can kneel and say simply, "Yes. I am guilty. I did it." We have many resources at our disposal to get rid of neurotic and pathological guilt, but only repentance and forgiveness can touch the real thing.

John Climacus (in the seventh century) called repentance "a contract with God for a fresh start in life. Repentance goes shopping for humility. Repentance is critical awareness and is the daughter of hope and the refusal to despair."[3] The point of repentance is to develop an intense awareness so that the truth may be told and seen. Lent is an opportunity to "go shopping for humility" and to dig deep into our lostness and with full critical awareness say, "I did it! *I* did it! I cannot blame anyone; not my parents, not my upbringing. I *did* it and I am sorry." When we do that, a new space opens up within us that was not there before. Repentance is an act of new creation by which new possibilities are offered us as a free gift. We finally get off the road that leads nowhere and find ourselves on the path home.

Taking our choices seriously means being willing to take on responsibility and giving up trying to negotiate with God for full or limited immunity in exchange for our pointing the finger at someone else. We finally come to the dead end of our negotiating ploys. We are nailed to the wall by a passionate love that takes us so seriously that it demands that we admit responsibility for our actions. We *are* guilty. We *are* forgiven.

The key to forgiveness is memory. We have to wake up and remember where we are, remember we are lost. We have, for example, during the past few years, been trying to remember accurately the Vietnam War. Some have tried to rewrite history. Others cannot yet bring themselves to remember. Yet there has been a growing realization that remembering and remembering truly is the key to healing and reconciliation. Only an act of remembrance can bring us back together. The idea for a Vietnam Memorial originated with a veteran going to see the movie *The Deer Hunter* in March of 1979. The movie upset him deeply. He was not only touched by the terrible actions of the war itself but angered by the nation as a whole for turning its back on the very young people who thought they were fighting for their country. When the war went sour, the country didn't want to know. At 3 A.M. the veteran found himself alone in the kitchen with a bottle of whiskey. Then the terrible flashbacks began in which he relived his experience of the war.

Pieces of bodies belonging to his friends were scattered in front of him. All he had was one first-aid bandage he pulled from his pocket. He screamed. When the flashbacks stopped, the faces of his comrades continued to pile up before his eyes. The names, he thought. The names. No one remembers their names!

Unless the names of the dead are remembered and our guilt acknowledged there can be no healing, no way back from the road that leads nowhere. The Vietnam Memorial marks the beginning of a healing for this nation with regard to its longest war. We are all called to acts of remembrance. Lent is a time for us to remember what we have done and to say, "Yes, I did it and I am sorry."

Robert Lowell, during a period of great personal upheaval, mental agony, and depression, confessed:

> *I am writing my autobiography literally "to pass the time." I almost doubt that time would pass otherwise. However, I also hope the result will supply me with swaddling clothes, with a sort of immense bandage of grace… for my hurt nerves.*

In an act of remembrance, he wove a bandage of grace for his hurts. He saw his most fundamental relationships in a new light. In a touching few words he remembered his father. "My own father was a gentle, faithful and dim man. I don't know why I was agin him. I hope there will be peace." The willingness to remember can open up new avenues of journeying. Our lives can take on a new direction.

The Holy Spirit drove Jesus into the wilderness to be tempted. The wilderness is the place of error, of lostness, of spiritual amnesia. It is also the place where a new way can be found by an act of memory. The desert is the place to recover our betrayed and lost dreams.

> *What happens to a dream deferred?*
> *Does it dry up like a raisin in the sun?*
> *Or fester, like a sore, then run?*

These words of Langston Hughes remind us of Martin Luther King's dream for this country—a dream still in the making, still unrealized. We are all guilty of not keeping the dream in mind. We forget and shift into fantasies of indifference or self-sufficiency. I find that I am more a man of the clock than of the dream. In fact, I am guilty of repressing my memory of the Great Dream of one human family in which no one is left out. St. Augustine dreamed of a road that would bring us all back together. The Way was and is Jesus Christ.

Adam means the whole earth. Once we were in a single place. Then we fell, were split into fragments and filled the whole earth. But the mercy of God collected the pieces from everywhere, melted them in the fire of his love, and fused together again what had been broken.

This is our dream that "broken bones may joy." It is a way of remembering, of finding our way back to the road that leads somewhere, which is risky and not safe and productive of long and dire consequences.

Am I making things more difficult than they really are? I don't think so. The promise of new space and new direction in our lives frightens as well as consoles us. "What we want most we avoid most" is a psychological truism. It is hard because our "heart's desire" is the last thing in the world we want! We prefer the tiny pond of the known and the familiar to the great oceans of new possibility a step or two away. We resist the offer of new space, because we are comforted by the constrictions of our present dead end. We reject going in another direction, because being nowhere has its compensations. It means that we are free of responsibility. We are stuck and, therefore, have been relieved of the burden of choice. We are in a kind of hell. It might not be much, but it feels like home. We are out of touch, but our blessed forgetfulness helps us to deny that we ever knew what it was to be in touch. On the whole our despair gives us a sense of satisfaction. Why open up old wounds? Why risk remembering? Why risk the welling up of feelings best left submerged? It is, however, a rule of the inner life that what is inside must come out. Our passions, our repressed memories and feelings, come out in addictive behavior, illnesses, acts of meanness and violence. We often say, "I don't know what came over me. I wasn't myself this morning." What comes over us is our lost and rejected self. If you listen carefully you can hear it crying out for healing.

John Updike, in his novel *Roger's Version*, describes an encounter between Roger Lambert and his niece, Verna. She is putting on an act and Roger thinks to himself:

> *More role-playing... and not especially well-played. Westerners have lost whole octaves of passion. Third world women can still make an inhuman piercing grieving noise right from the floor of the soul, as you can see and hear on television clips from Lebanon and Ethiopia.*[4]

Is that the nearest we can get to a reminder of the passion stirring in the depths of our souls? Television clips remind us of what we have lost—whole octaves of passion. Where should we look for these lost octaves? Without them, our music is thin, and the song we sing, a wail or a whine with no ground. The road to recovery lies between what the Christian tradition calls the Old Adam and the New, between the narrow confines of the old and the hope-bearing possibilities of the new. Lost passion is recovered insofar as we are willing to be stretched between the two.

Imagine your mother being pregnant with you. Imagine her coming to term. Recovering lost octaves of passion is like that. It is being penetrated by the new and being made pregnant with it. Years ago, a new fact came into existence: you! The same energy that made the sun and the stars came into play, and the result was you. You matter and your choices matter. If you lose sight of that, you get frozen and lost. You are not an accident. To discover that is already to have recovered enough passion to turn you away from a dead end and toward life. Affirming that you are not an accident is to affirm that you have a purpose, a mission in life. Your most important task is to find out what that mission is. One of the most quoted verses from the New Testament affirms the fact that you matter: "God loved the world so much that he gave his only Son, that everyone who has faith in him may not die but have eternal life" (John 3:16, NEB). The recovery of passion is the recovery of the accurate view of ourselves as God's joy, as God's delight. We are "the apple of God's eye." We forget that. We get lost. We come to a dead end.

The recovery of passion involves a way of remembering. It is as if we have to turn back on the road and find our way to the point along the path where we first got lost. We are able, then, to take a step in the right direction when we accept both the burden of guilt and the risk of responsibility. In short, when we take guilt and responsibility seriously we begin to take ourselves seriously. We are not accidents. We accept responsibility for our actions. We repent of our sins and find that we are under no condemnation. We are pushed by grace in the direction of grace.

Our society, however, offers to provide us with too easy means of defining ourselves and our mission in the world. A maze of roads, each one promising to be the path to happiness, confronts us. We easily get lost in a labyrinth of wild promises that appeal to our greed and our insecurity. One such "wild promise" came to our mail box not long ago in the form of a large envelope. It was delivered with the junk mail and was from "American Family Publishers." The word *family* on the envelope sounded reassuring. I opened the envelope and was promised heaven in the form of not only a fortune but also an opportunity to appear on TV with Ed McMahon. Through the window on the envelope were these words in large print: THE NIGHT WHEN ALAN JONES WON TEN MILLION DOLLARS. My ten-year-old son was mesmerized by this miracle.

"Let's mail it in, Dad!"

"All right," I said, "But if I win I'll have to appear on TV with Ed McMahon. I'm not sure I want to do that. Anyway, I'd want to give it all away."

My son looked at me as if I'd gone mad. To humor me, he said, "OK, but let's keep a million."

"Sure!" I said, but he could see that I had a faraway look in my eye. I was thinking of Ed and me on TV. It is not really my idea of heaven, but it seems to be the vision shared by many of my contemporaries. The blurb went like this: "The script begins with Alan Jones' childhood. It includes the town where you were born. It talks about the courageous times 'before you won the big money.' It shows the present Alan Jones against the backdrop of San Francisco." I liked the bit about the "courageous times."

I wonder what the TV script writers would have done with my somewhat pedestrian life (at least to outward appearances) in order to give it a little glamor? I am very attracted to the idea of having someone rewrite my life, beginning with my being the bastard son of a Russian prince who abandoned my mother and came back full of guilt and remorse (and very rich) to reclaim us out of abject poverty! I didn't dare mail it in. Given our contemporary values, I thought that, not only might I win, but I *should*. I am, after all, very religious, and religion is supposed to pay off in material terms in our culture. Who knows, perhaps being very rich and being on TV is my mission?

It didn't take long to come to the dead end of that particular road. The music was unusually thin. Whole octaves of passion had been lost. But there are paths even more seductive. Many roads announce that they lead to freedom, but a dead end awaits the unwary traveller. Sexual freedom, for example, is a fire that burns more people than it transforms. Unbridled individualism unhinges many of us into imagining that freedom is doing what one wants when one wants to do it. The most deadly road is often a religious one. Those who take it in the hope of finding easy answers rather than the mystery of grace can do a great deal of harm to themselves and to others.

Finding the true road means facing hard questions. They open up a new space inside us and give a new direction to our lives. We are made to face hard questions in areas where we hoped to be left alone. We are touched in that place that is sacrosanct for most of us—in the deep place of the heart where passion is born. As one commentator put it, there is no private life any more: "Suddenly sex is a very public political issue. The country is pondering how the most intimate acts are inextricably social; how millions of personal choices affect the common good."[5]

Our choices *matter*. Even the little ones can have far-reaching consequences. There is no such thing as a private act. There may be acts that we perform in private, but everything we do, even the most intimate and private, affects everyone and everything else. The function of the Church is to keep alive our ability to see and to make choices. Sometimes the Church embarrasses us by nailing us to the wall and insisting that what we do really matters. The Church does not so much threaten us with the possibility of punishment as hold out in love the burden of meaning and significance. Lost notes in the scale of passion need to be restored, and restoration begins with turning away from irresponsibility, which is a thin disguise for the destructive belief that we are of no importance. If we matter then what we do matters. Because I am not an accident but a human being with a purpose, a mission in the world. I cannot behave as I please and expect it not to make any difference. Of course it makes a difference how we behave! It makes a difference because we are loved and because we matter.

We find our way home by recovering the Passion at the center of every human life. As we have seen, repentance is the name of that struggle. Repentance is admitting that we are on a road leading nowhere. St. Augustine describes the process movingly in Book 8 of his *Confessions*:

> *I probed the hidden depths of my soul and wrung its pitiful secrets from it, and when I mustered them all before the eyes of my heart, a great storm broke within me, bringing with it a great deluge of tears.*
>
> *...Somehow I flung myself down beneath a fig-tree and gave way to the tears which now streamed from my eyes, the sacrifice that is acceptable to you... in my misery I kept crying, "How long shall I go on saying, 'tomorrow, tomorrow.' Why not now?"*[6]

Augustine then heard a child in a nearby house say over and over again, "Take it and read, Take it and read." He then opened his copy of St. Paul's Epistles and read these words: "Not in reveling and drunkenness, not in lust and wantonness, not in quarrels and rivalries. Rather, arm yourselves with the Lord Jesus Christ; spend no more thought on nature and nature's appetites" (Rom. 13:13, 14). These verses opened Augustine's heart. Why not now? is the question repentance always poses. Why not turn away from the dead end in which you find yourself and make the pilgrimage home?

Later in his *Confessions* (Book 10.27), Augustine is a lover who has come home to his beloved.

> *How late I came to love you, O beauty so ancient and so fresh, how late I came to love you! You were within me, while I had gone outside to seek you. Unlovely myself, I rushed towards all those lovely things you had made. And always you were with me, and I was not with you… You called, you cried, you shattered my deafness. You sparkled, you blazed, you drove away my blindness. You shed your fragrance, and I drew in my breath, and I pant for you. I tasted and I now hunger and thirst. You touched me, and I now burn with longing for your peace.*[7]

Repentance insists that the time is now, the time is for lovers. Repentance is the word of hope saying, "Yes! Come and live!" But the way back to the right path is different for everyone. We have our own peculiar route even though we are all on the same journey. Richard Baxter in 1696 wrote, after his conversion, "But I understand that God breaketh not all men's hearts alike…"[8] Repentance is for lovers. It is for the enlarging of the heart. Ours then, is a struggle to recover lost octaves of passion so that we may be truer and better lovers. Our souls long for a love that is hard not soft, risky not safe; a love that is productive of long and dire consequences. No wonder we delay! We want this kind of love, but we're not sure we want it now. Why not now? Why not take the hand that is offered us to climb out of our particular "hell"? The reason is that, while we do not like where we are, at least the dead end in which we find ourselves is familiar. We have even begun to think of it as home.

Not long ago two cartoons appeared in the *New Yorker*. Both depicted the Devil welcoming a new contingent of souls to hell. In one, the Devil, with a smile, says, "It's OK. There's no right and wrong here. It's what works for you!" In the other, the Devil is saying, "Just try to think of hell as a sort of support group for the eternally damned." We have an enormous capacity for making ourselves at home in the most damnable of places and for accommodating ourselves to the most degrading social and political compromises. It is a great sacrifice to give up the safety of our little encampments on the road and respond to our passion for pilgrimage. Hear the words of God trying to reach you: "I sparkle, I blaze, I drive away your blindness. You matter. What you do makes a difference. Your choices will make the future and each choice for good, however small, wins strategic ground against the enemy." Evil is a serious thing. It is that which brings us to nothing and freezes us in immobility. While the voice of life says, "The time is now!" the voice of death whispers, "Why bother?" Hell is the metaphor for this frozen immobility. It seductively suggests that there is no journey. The hellishness of hell is that it is a "no-place" of ice-cold paralysis. Augustine fought his conversion because he found it incredible that God should seek him out and passionately love him. Like Augustine, we are easily seduced into finding the displacement and immobility more real than love.

The symptoms of our sickness are obvious when we make the wrong choice and opt for the stiffness and rigidity of being no-place. They are the classic sins of pride, lying, and despair. These are the sins of separation. Pride cuts us off from love; lying, from truth; and despair, from mercy. All three see to it that we freeze to death. They make sure that nothing new can move in us. The ice they produce makes sure that there can be no fresh space, no new direction in our lives. The spirit that rules over hell says, "I am the door that is forever closed, the road that leads nowhere."

The challenge of the gospel is, Will you allow your drifting to be consecrated into pilgrimage? Will you entertain the possibility that you matter, that you are here for a purpose, that you have a mission that no one else can fulfill? How far do you pay attention to the voice that whispers, "Follow me. I am the door that is forever shut. I am the road that leads to nowhere"?[9]

There are two wonderful stories in the Bible, one in the Old Testament and the other in the New, that give us two signs or weapons against pride, lying, and despair. The first sign is that of Abraham and Sarah, an old couple "as good as dead." God makes of them a new beginning for the world. He says to them, "Go from your country and your kindred and your father's house to the land that I will show you" (Gen. 12:1–8, RSV). Go out into the wilderness of untried things, to the place not of safety but of risk. Take a new path. Find a fresh space for you and your people. Through you, you who are as good as dead, the nations of the world will be blessed." Abraham and Sarah, "as good as dead," are signs to us that a new beginning is always possible.

The second sign, taken from the New Testament (John 3:1–17), is of a newborn baby in contrast to Abraham and Sarah. Nicodemus goes to see Jesus under the cover of darkness to receive a healing word. Jesus says to him, "Unless one is born anew, he cannot see the kingdom of God." Our escape from the road that leads nowhere depends on our willingness to be born anew. It is a great pity that the wonderful phrase "to be born again" has become so overused in our society as to render it almost meaningless. Many not only claim to be "born again" but also make their particular interpretation of it the criterion by which all other would-be believers are judged. New birth is essential in the spiritual life. It is a process that never ends. New space opens up in us, and a new direction is given to our lives insofar as we are willing to be born anew.

The two great signs against the power of evil in this world are an elderly couple and a newborn baby. The faithfulness of old age and the simplicity of a baby are part of the armor of those who would go on pilgrimage. We find a strength beyond our imaginings in our willingness, powerless as we are, to go together, hand in hand, into the wilderness of untried things. It is in that wilderness we recover lost octaves of passion. It is in faithfulness and simplicity we understand that we, and all those with whom we share life on this planet, matter.

We leave the road that leads nowhere fortified by two signs: two old people, called to leave home; and a newborn baby. The wonder is that these two signs are, not only ones *from* God, but also signs *of* God. God is a pilgrim, journeying with us. God is a baby, vulnerable and helpless. As we approach the mystery of Good Friday, we shall see God is the Crucified One. The road home is through the desert of powerlessness beyond which is the High Road home.

We have come to a dead end. We, like Abraham and Sarah, are as good as dead. Imagine: you *are* Abraham, you *are* Sarah, you *are* Nicodemus. Allow these Bible stories to become the blueprint for the adventure of your own soul. Let the images take root in you, to make space, to give you new direction. Your own soul is a vast desert for your homecoming. It is full of holy places of encounter with God.

The abbot of the Coptic Monastery of St. Macarius in the Egyptian desert was asked whether he intended to make a pilgrimage to the Holy Land. While he revered the Holy Land, he felt that he had no need to go there.

> *Jerusalem, the Holy, is right here, in and around these caves; for what else is my cave, but the place where my savior Christ was born; what else is my cave, but the place where he most gloriously rose again from the dead. Jerusalem is here, right here, and all the spiritual riches of the holy city are found in this wadi.*

Another monk said, "The monk's cell is the furnace of Babylon, in which the three children found the Son of God; it is the pillar of cloud from which God spoke to Moses."

When we come to a dead end on the road that leads nowhere,

we have to wait in our cave, in our cell, until we are given a new direction. There is nowhere to go. Our only choice is to wait. Lent is one of the times to be in your cave, the place of your becoming, the place of pregnancy. When we move, we journey with Abraham and Sarah through the murky regions of our anxiety and shame, and through our various wanderings we love and lose each other.

I find that I come up against a fundamental question that is hard for me to answer. Is anyone or anything really to be trusted? I find it difficult to trust. I want to trust my fellow pilgrims, but I rarely do. Trust is something that has to be freely given. I need to give it to you and you to me. We have to learn to trust each other even as we betray each other. This is part of our pain. Trust is a gift, and the miracle of faith is this: God, our fellow pilgrim, trusts us. God believes in us. God has faith in us. It is God's faithfulness that enables us to have faith. Faith is the acceptance that we are trusted, that God believes in us. It is God's "amazing grace" that melts the ice around the heart and rescues us from our spiritual immobility. It is God's love that so moves in us that we are able to resist the forces of resentment in the world.

Our world aches to be warmed back to life. The frozen heart is thawed a little every time we reach out to one another. What else do we have to give each other, friends and enemies alike, except ourselves? Abraham, Sarah, and Nicodemus are our companions. We share a common journey. Isn't it time that your drifting was consecrated into pilgrimage? You have a mission. You are needed. The road that leads nowhere has to be abandoned. The Road to Calvary is the road home, and we are already on it. It is a road for joyful pilgrims intent on the recovery of passion.

Christian, in *Pilgrim's Progress*, follows the road to the foot of the cross. John Bunyan wrote:

> *So I saw in my dream, that just as Christian came up to the Cross, his burden loosed from off his shoulders, and fell from off his back; and began to tumble, and so continued to do till it came to the mouth of the sepulchre, where it fell in, and I saw it no more.*

> *Then was Christian glad and lightsome, and said with a merry heart, "He hath given me rest, by his sorrow, and life, by his death..." Then Christian gave three leaps of joy, and went on singing.*[10]

The Road to Calvary, however, doesn't sound like the way home. We will find ourselves at the foot of the cross eventually. We will have reason to leap for joy. But there are other adventures ahead of us before we are ready for "the place of the skull."

Study Questions

1. "The unpalatable truth is that it is possible to get lost... Our choices matter" (p. 26). This realization and the acceptance of the consequences of our actions lead to repentance, which brings new possibilities. What examples can you name of losing our way, corporately or individually? What changes has repentance demanded? At what cost?

2. Jones writes of the truism that "what we want most we avoid most," and that "our lost and rejected self" cries out for healing. Do you experience these things as true? What enables you to stretch yourself beyond the known and the familiar?

3. In the struggle "to recover lost octaves of passion," we fight against the classic sins of pride, lying, and despair. What suggestions does Jones offer to aid us in that fight? What promises keep us struggling?

4. What does Jones suggest are the two great signs against the power of evil in this world? (See p. 37.) What do they show us?

3.
Home—The Last Place on Earth

The Christian life is an adventure. Thinking of life as an adventure is nothing new. At one time or another we may dream about going on one. We long for something to take us out of this present moment and catapult us into the realm of marvel and wonder. An adventure can mean many things. It can start with a stroke of luck, an accident, or a random event. And it's not all fun and romance. To be involved in one could mean that one's life hangs in the balance. There are often trials, dangers, the possibility of loss, and the risk of failure. One has to be prepared to face perils, to perform daring feats, and to lay one's life on the line. An adventure could lead to the last place on earth, to the point of no return. In a serious adventure the outcome is not a foregone conclusion.

The reason we avoid the adventurous is not so much that we fear the dangers but rather that we do not want to be let down. We know from experience that life is not a series of "highs" following one after the other in endless variation. Life is sometimes plodding and boring. That may be why many people live in the past. Paul Tournier writes, "I have seen many people who will even go so far as to lie to themselves rather than admit that they are disappointed." He gives the example of the person who was once alive in the Spirit but who cannot maintain the feelings of warmth and spontaneity. This person gradually slipped into a life of habit and mediocrity.

We throw in the towel because we do not know the rules of the game. We do not understand the adventure in which we find ourselves. Tournier points out

> *in spiritual matters nothing is preserved, nothing can be saved up. [We mistake] a psychological problem for a religious one. [We refuse] to recognize the law of adventure, which is that it dies as it achieves its object. The first requirement of religion is that we accept the laws of life. The spiri-*

*tual life consists only in a series of new births. There must be
new flowerings, new prophets, new adventures—if the heart
of man, albeit in fits and starts, is to go on beating.*[1]

What is true for individual human beings is true for institutions
as well. The Church is the place of adventure, although one wouldn't
always think so. Religion is often a pallid affair. In fact, the word *affair*
is a good way to describe it. For many, religion is like a love affair gone
sour. The adventure goes out of it, and we are left with a kind of routine boredom. For many people religion is not so much dead as something that was never alive in the first place. Some blame secularism
and a general antireligious attitude for the eclipse of religion in modern society. Abraham Joshua Heschel maintained that "it would be
more honest to blame religion for its own defeats." He goes on:

*Religion declined not because it was refuted, but because it
became irrelevant, dull, oppressive, stupid. When faith is
completely replaced by creed, worship by discipline, love by
habit; when the crisis of today is ignored because of the splendor of the past; when faith becomes an heirloom rather than
a living fountain; when religion speaks only in the name of
authority rather than with the voice of compassion—its
message becomes meaningless.*[2]

Religion becomes meaningless when we lose touch with our
longings, when we fail to see life as an adventure, when we refuse
to imagine that each one of us has a mission. It is as if we live with
the ache of a memory of an adventure that won't go away. We find
the road to the adventure of the spirit by struggling with memory.
A word or look from a friend, a tragic or joyful event, a smell, a
particular place, often jolt the memory. They remind us of what
has been disclosed to us human beings through the ages about the
meaning of our longing. These reminders (writes Heschel)

*are hanging over our souls like stars, remote and of mind-
surpassing grandeur. They shine through the dark and dan-*

gerous ages, and their reflection can be seen in the lives of those who guard the path of conscience and memory in the wilderness of careless living.[3]

We wander in the wilderness of careless living looking for home. If we pay attention to the deep ache in us, which memory stirs up, we shall lose our complacency and security. The lying voice that says "I am come that you might have safety and have it more abundantly" no longer has any power in a place where we sense we are pregnant with something new and enormous.

We are meant to find our true home in God, and that means undergoing a series of new births. In a sense we never arrive. Never to arrive is a strange definition of "home." Home is the place we never reach. It is the last place on earth. Yet it is a place that is always available to us. It is, at once, elusive and in our hearts. How is this so?

From the perspective of the mystics, a human being is, by definition, "a longing for God." The whole aim of the spiritual life is to keep that longing alive. When that dies we die. We are defined by our longings, and since we will never feel "at home" until we rest in God, we shall never be satisfied. If God is our "home" how could we ever hope to reach it? Far from being a reason to despair, the mystics saw the inexhaustible mystery of God as our real hope, because no boundaries can be set on our pilgrimage home. St. Gregory of Nyssa, at the end of the fourth century, wrote, "No limit can be set on our progress towards God: first because no limitation can be put upon the beautiful, and secondly because the increase in our desire for the beautiful cannot be stopped by any sense of satisfaction."[4]

"Home" becomes both a metaphor for our longings that will never be satisfied *and* the promise of our being truly at home with ourselves in God even while we are on pilgrimage.

As we have seen, Allan Bloom insists that education is a matter of longing and passion. It is an erotic adventure. But our eroticism is wounded. What Bloom writes about students applies to us all. We are impoverished in our longing and devoid of imagination when it comes to our reaching out to others.

> [*Students*] *are adult in the sense that they will no longer change very much. They may become competent specialists, but they are flat-souled. The world is for them what it presents itself to the senses to be; it is unadorned by imagination and devoid of ideals. This flat soul is what the sexual wisdom of our time conspires to make universal... A trip to Florence is one thing for a young man who hopes to meet his Beatrice on the Ponte Santa Trinita... it is quite another who goes without such an aching need... Such longing is what most students need.*[5]

I know I need to live out of the depths of my aching and longing, but I am reluctant to do so. The promise of a fiery ordeal makes me want to give up. The agenda of the adventure is too heavy, too serious. Its express purpose is to push us more deeply into things than we would care to go. But given the shallowness of our lives, something drives us to dig deeper even as we hesitate.

The pilgrimage to Easter bombards us with metaphors of extremity. If we take it seriously, we will be pushed to the edge. A voice inside our heads will insist that it is all an exaggeration. Things can't be that bad. Nothing can be that important. Yet here we are, peering over the edge, looking at the reality of our guilt, at the reality of our connivance at and complicity in the general fallenness and messiness of things. We even have to look at our capacity for evil. This is all too much and all for what? A "homecoming" that is at the heart of a consuming fire! This is a passion beyond our comprehension. There is the possibility of real suffering. There is no such thing as a risk-free, hassle-free adventure. This kind of talk can be easily misunderstood. One hears a lot of superficial chat about Christian or Jewish religious "masochism." Christians and Jews are supposed to be "into" suffering. There are horror stories (many of them true) of strict religious practices that have frightened people away from religion altogether. No doubt there can be an unhealthy interest in suffering. There is also a kind of suffering that is a terrible mystery. It presents us with a black hole of meaninglessness. Sometimes heroic souls tear meaning from it, but often it sits there as a gaping wound. I do not understand it. There is, however, a kind of suffering that I do understand. In the context of the human adventure there is a species of suffering that is to be expected. It is normal. It is the suffering that accompanies growth. We suffer when we are stretched, when our minds are expanded and our hearts broken so that they may be enlarged. One of the most powerful metaphors of spiritual suffering is that of thirst. Our longing in the wilderness is spoken of as a longing for water. In Exodus (17:1-7) the people's longing for water was combined with their grumbling and complaining against Moses. The adventure turned out to be a great disappointment.

But the people thirsted for water, and the people murmured against Moses, and said, "Why did you bring us out of Egypt, to kill us and our children and our cattle with thirst?" (Exod. 17:3, RSV)

Moses struck the rock, and the waters gushed out. Moses named the place Massah and Meribah "because of the faultfinding of the children of Israel, and because they put the Lord to the proof by saying, 'Is the Lord among us or not?'"

The desert, the last place on earth, turns out to be (in spite of all our discontent and self-pity) the place of living water. The desert is a symbol of two things: human extremity and God's self-giving. We need to be jolted out of our apparent self-sufficiency into the place of real need so that God can give himself to us. We need to be introduced to our longings, because they guard our mystery. Simone Weil wrote:

At the bottom of every human being, from the earliest infancy until the tomb, there is something that goes on indomitably expecting, in the teeth of all experience of crimes committed, suffered and witnessed, that good and not evil will be done to him. It is this above all that is sacred in every human being.

How far do we ache for the sacred within us? Have we lost our taste for it? Do we thirst for it?

There is no theme more important in this adventure than that of the Exodus. Our life is a great pilgrimage away from chaos and death into a fullness of life. John Donne, the dean of St. Paul's Cathedral in the seventeenth century, used the Exodus theme in his personal devotions. "As thou has enlightened and enlarged me to contemplate thy greatness, so, O God, descend and stoop down to see my infirmities and the Egypt in which I live, and (if thy good pleasure be such) hasten mine Exodus and deliverance." In another prayer he wrote: "But, O God, as mine inward corruptions have made me my own Pharoah and mine own Egypt, so thou, by the inhabitation of thy Spirit, and application of thy merit, hast made me my own Christ; and contenting thyself with being my medicine, allowest me to be my own physician."

John Donne took the image of the Exodus and applied it, through a powerful act of the imagination, to his own life. That image illuminates our own pilgrimage as surely as it enlightened his. It enlarges our hearts to breaking point as it did his. The biblical images have the power to change and catapult us into adventure inasmuch as we allow them to take root in us. The desert is the place where this happens. We have to go to the place of extremity. The adventure really begins here in the desert, "the last place on earth."

In 1788, "the last place on earth" was Australia. At least the English thought so. That is where they sent their outcasts, their shadowy and unacceptable brothers and sisters. Every society has a last place on earth, a place of exile, a place to send people and then forget about them. At the end of the eighteenth century the English sent thieves, whores, and highwaymen to Australia.[6] The secret and terrible thought of many today is, if only we had such a place to send the homeless on our streets, people with AIDS, the mentally ill, and the socially unacceptable. Let us send them into the desert, to the last place on earth. We could even congratulate ourselves in being humane. Exile, after all, is a cut above extermination. The adventure we are on, however, does not permit us to exile anyone. We are, after all, in exile ourselves. Ours is a pilgrimage of compassion, which means that there is no place we can send others without our going along with them. If we send people off to the last place on earth, we find ourselves bound with them as fellow passengers on the boat to the Botany Bay of the spirit. We are companions of the very people we would reject and rather forget. We are not, after all, a band of high-class pilgrims. Our companions are "excrementitious outcasts" (to use Jeremy Bentham's phrase). We find ourselves in fellowship with what we most despise and fear. Why? So that we might penetrate the terrible mystery of how our "decency" is often purchased at the expense of someone else's humiliation. It is hardly surprisingly that we would rather not go on this kind of adventure. It is, however, too late. We are here at the last place on earth in the company of all those who are the enemies of our imagined peace and happiness. We, all of us together, are at the end of our endurance. We are all having to live with our ache and our longing, but, dying of thirst, we don't know where to turn.

What would be good news for those who were dying of thirst? Water from the Rock! One of our wretched companions in the desert place is the cynic whose bitterness acknowledges our longing while insisting that no remedy or rescue is at hand. The cynic insists that nothing hopeful or new could originate in us. The rock to which we seem chained holds no hidden spring. A character in Iris Murdoch's novel *The Good Apprentice* bitingly observes, "You need some lessons in psychology. The fact about human nature is that things are indelible. Religion is a lie because it pretends you can start again. That's what made Christianity so popular."[7] The cynic is a liar. The desert where the living water is is the place of new beginnings. True, it is also the place where we have to give up our illusions. Such a giving up feels like death. The desert is the place where, in the company of those we have come to despise, we learn to say, "I'm sorry." It is the place where we face hard questions concerning our own guilt and our capacity for and connivance with evil. It is the place of truth. The psychiatrist in *The Good Apprentice* tells his patient who finds himself at the last place on earth,

Truthful remorse leads to the fruitful death of the self, not to its survival as a successful liar. Recognize lies and reject them

at every point... Move beyond them into an open and quiet
area which you will find to be an entirely new place. You
have never been in such a place before and the person who is
there is a new person... We are forced to choose between
some painful recognition of truth and an ever more aggres-
sive manufacturing of lies.[8]

The pilgrimage we are on together involves the death of the
self that would like to survive as a successful liar. If we go through
that death, we find a new world.

Broken bones may joy, and their mending begins here in the
desert, the last place on earth. Our passion for pilgrimage has
brought us to a place of a kind of suffering that is normal for those
who call themselves human and want to live the truth and not a
lie. The imperative of this desert is, give up the lying and pretense.
Embrace a kind of suffering and discover a new place to *be*! Here
we can plumb the depths of our ache and longing by making the
journey into the second infinity, which is our own sacred mystery.
We experience suffering when we accept our limitations, the limitations of form, of time and place.

Our companions, the attractive and the unattractive, confront us
with the crippling and infantile character of our sense of boundless-
ness and omnipotence. Our immaturity is shown up for what it is
when we rage against the fact that freedom does not mean doing anything we want—with no strings and no restrictions. As we progress
on the pilgrimage, the mystery of human freedom lies in doing what
we *have* to do! We do what we *must* do, but from a new place inside
ourselves that has surrendered to God and to nothing and to no one
else. We find that we can do our duty not out of duty but out of love.

Why all this? Our suffering on pilgrimage is for the revivify-
ing, cleansing, and clarifying of our longings. It shows us their true
object. The deepest of our aches was put there by love. We cannot
help being lovers. St. Augustine put it beautifully.

Love cannot be idle. What is it that moves absolutely anyone,
even to do evil, if it is not love? Show me a love that is idle

and doing nothing. Scandals, adulteries, crimes, murders, every kind of excess, are they not the work of love? Cleanse your loves then. Divert into the garden the water that was running down the drain. Am I telling you not to love anything? Far from it! If you do not love anything you will be dolts, dead, despicable creatures. Love by all means, but take care what it is you love.

We brought to the last place on earth for the clarifying and cleansing of our loving. We find ourselves in the middle of a Passion Play, a love story. When we shrink from embarking on this pilgrimage, we delay (again and again) our entry into the desert of new beginnings. We have an appointment to keep on Good Friday. Calvary is the Hill of God's Passion. The place where God, like a mother, goes into labor for our new birth.

There's a story about H. H. Kelly, S.S.M. (1860–1950), an English monk who founded a religious community and a seminary. He was known for his fierce insistence on the sovereignty and priority of God. God is all in all. One day a student was brave enough to challenge Father Kelly and ask, "If God is really sovereign and does everything, why do we need to bother?" The old man offered the stunning reply, "If you don't *do* something you may miss your crucifixion, and that would be a pity!" Such an affirmation, as we have seen, can be easily misunderstood as an encouragement to masochism. Father Kelly meant that our only response to the passionate love of God for us is a passionate response. Passion is a special kind of suffering. The old monk believed in it. He would watch the students play soccer and yell at any of them who failed to play with every ounce of his being, "You don't love God enough!" This was his approach to every aspect of the students' life. He once wrote on a student's term paper, which was carelessly researched and sloppily written, "This essay shows nothing of the love of God!" He did not mean that it lacked pious thoughts but that its sloppy presentation betrayed a lack of passion.

Learning to love is tough business at the best of times. When we are in the desert, at the last place on earth, with the kind of company we're in, it is doubly difficult. Our helplessness and our frailty become our best weapons. Graham Greene's novel *A Burnt-Out Case* tells the story of a successful architect (Querry) who abandons his career and goes deep into the Congo, which, for him, is the last place on earth. He has come to the end of his rope and lost the will to live. He finds a way to serve people and yet feels nothing for them. At the furthest point of his reluctant pilgrimage he stops at a leper colony. It is there, at the end of the world, that he begins to recover his passion. He is asked to design and oversee the construction of a hospital. He writes to the doctor at the leper colony,

> *A vocation is an act of love: it is not a professional career. When desire is dead one cannot continue to make love. I've come to the end of desire and to the end of vocation. Don't try to bind me in a loveless marriage and to make me imitate what I used to perform with passion. And don't talk to me like a priest about my duty. A talent… should not be buried when it still has purchasing power, but when the currency has changed and the image has been superseded and no value is left in the coin but the weight of a wafer of silver, a man has every right to hide it. Obsolete coins, like corn, have always been found in graves.*[9]

Here is a man, like Abraham and Sarah, as good as dead, who has come to the last place on earth. Near the end of the book, Querry (a bottle of whiskey in hand) tells a parable about the elusiveness of God and the pain of love to the wife of a local factory manager. Parables have the power to heal, and through the telling of the story, Querry slowly realizes where he is on his pilgrimage and gradually accepts the mysterious grace operating even at the last place on earth. The parable concerns a young man who grows up to be a successful jeweler. When he was a boy, his parents told him "stories about the King who lived in a city a hundred miles away—about the distance of the furthest star." The King knew everything and watched over everyone. The boy grew up and married. His only child died. In the end he became a successful jeweler and lover. "He left his wife and his mistress, he left a lot of women, but he always had a great deal of fun with them first. They called it love and so did he." He continued to prosper in spite of the fact of his unfaithful heart.

The only trouble was that he became bored, more and more bored. Nobody ever seemed to say no to him. Nobody ever made him suffer—it was always other people who suffered. Sometimes just for a change he would have welcomed the feeling the pain of punishment that the King must all the time have been inflicting on him.[10]

One day he made a terrible discovery. He realized that for all his lovemaking he did not really know what love was. He had to admit that he didn't love anyone or anything. To make matters worse, the jeweler came to the conclusion that he was no real artist either. He was only a clever jeweler, a mere technician. He "had got to the end of pleasure just as now he had got to the end of work." The strange thing was that he experienced this coming to the end of things as a kind of relief. He had "come clean" at last. There was a flood of grace. His loss of love and work led to the loss of his belief in the King. Belief in himself and in the King seemed to go together. His loss of belief, however, was a kind of blessing. It was a relief to come to the "end" of love and work as ways of proving to himself that he was alive. There

were moments when he wondered if his unbelief were not after all a final and conclusive proof of the King's existence. This total vacancy might be his punishment for the rules he had wilfully broken. It was even possible that this is what people meant by pain.

The chapter ends with these words. "He thought, the King is dead, long live the King. Perhaps he had found here a country and a life."[11] This is the dark but liberating experience of those who have a passion for pilgrimage. We are in the company not only of

others we have rejected but, just as important, of the self we fear
and despise. Our way home is by way of the last place on earth,
because that is where we have exiled the dregs of our wounded self.
These rejected bits and pieces must first be gathered up before we
can continue our pilgrimage. God's passion for us is such that God
wants every part of us to come home.

STUDY QUESTIONS

1. Jones says, "The Christian life is an adventure," and "In a serious adventure the outcome is not a foregone conclusion" (p.
   41). How do these assertions interplay with your longing for
   safety? With your hope for something new?

2. What two things does Jones suggest are symbolized by the
   desert? (See p. 45.) What function do they serve? How have
   you experienced the desert in your own life, literally as well as
   symbolically?

3. Jones comments that "freedom does not mean doing anything
   we want—with no strings and no restrictions," but rather
   comes "in doing what we *have* to do… from a new place inside
   ourselves…" Is this sense of freedom familiar to you? In what
   other ways might freedom be defined? Look up "freedom" in
   a dictionary.

4. Jones cites Father Kelly as meaning that "our only response to
   the passionate love of God for us is a passionate response" (p.
   49). How does this call for passion relate to a life of spiritual
   discipline? In what ways is the experience of such passion
   dark? In what ways is it liberating?

4.
THE SEARCH FOR LIGHT

The road home leads to the last place on earth but does not stop there. We are brought to what we think is the end of the road only to find that a new path opens up in front of us. Sometimes I find myself believing that the dead end is all there is. I feel trapped and in the dark. The water is rising, and I begin to panic. I get frightened. I lose control. I lash out at others. I am terrified of being carried away, of drowning.

In her novel *The Nice and the Good*, Iris Murdoch places a supercilious and proud lawyer (Ducane) at the supreme place of risk. He is trapped in Gunnar's Cave near the seashore, and the tide is rising. He had gone off in search of a young man (Pierce) who, in his distress and grief-stricken self-importance, had swum there to drown. It did not take Pierce long to regret his decision to die. With her usual precision, Murdoch documents the motions of the human heart as passion (like the sea) rises and falls inside it. Inside Pierce "humiliation and rejection and despair had blended into a thrust of desire… Only Pierce had not realized that he would have to make *choices*. The idea of a choice brought with it the idea of life, of future, and this brought the first wrench of fear." The unwelcome but longed-for light of serious choice had uncovered his deep desire to live. But now the water was rising. It was too late for second thoughts.

Ducane swam into the cave and thought of Alice in *Through the Looking Glass* swimming with the mouse in the Pool of Tears. He thought, "In this sort of darkness I could pass within a yard of the way to safety and not know. It's all chance, utter chance."

I wonder if this is the end… and if so what will it all have amounted to. How tawdry and small it has all been. He saw himself now as a little rat, a busy little scurrying rat, seeking out its own little advantages and comforts. To live easily, to have cosy familiar pleasures, to be well thought of… He

thought, if I ever get out of here I will be no man's judge.
Nothing is worth doing except to kill the little rat, not to
judge, not to be superior, not to exercise power, not to seek,
seek, seek. To love and to reconcile and to forgive, only this
matters. All power is sin and all law is frailty. Love is the only
justice. Forgiveness, reconciliation, not law.[1]

The cynic might dismiss the evidence for what really matters
in life from a man who thought he was about to die, but I have
more confidence in the feelings of people placed at the extremities
of life than in those who are drugged by the comforts of the cozy
and familiar. There is a kind of light shining at the edge of things.
When we place ourselves at the center the light goes out. Our ego-
centrism is a great darkness. Something moves in me when I come
to the end of my rope, when I have exhausted my bag of tricks and
I have nothing left with which to negotiate. New life stirs in me
when my manipulative skills cut no ice. A light burns and shines
in my soul when I am pinned to the wall. It is in such moments
that I know that "to love and to reconcile and to forgive, only this
matters." It is in such moments that "I" begin to happen in new
and unexpected ways. When I find myself *in extremis*, a new light
begins to dawn. What I thought was the "end" is not the end after all.

In January 1986 there was an event that left a whole nation
grief-stricken. The space shuttle *Challenger* exploded in a blinding
flash of light. Many watched that sunburst of radiance on TV and
saw it descend into the sea. This tragedy became a light illuminating everything. Insofar as it captured the popular imagination, the
terrible death of the *Challenger's* crew became the prism through
which millions of people (at least for a few hours) saw the whole
of life in its frailty and preciousness.

Many such candles light up our world and make us see things
we would rather not see. We would prefer to remain in the dark. It
is as if tragedy makes darkness visible. The explosion of the space
shuttle was a burning candle none of us could ignore. We all
bathed in its light, and we saw each other in a new way. Other candles shine in a war-torn world. Terrorists light them all the time.

There are candles of hate as well as candles of love; candles that bring a healing light and ones that show us a wounding darkness. I don't like being awakened. I would prefer to live with just enough light to move around in my little world. An unadventuresome half-light would do. I want to avoid dark caves on the seashore where the tides can be treacherous.

A character in Walker Percy's *The Moviegoer* expresses this mood exactly. "It's not a bad thing to settle for the little ways; not the big search for the big happiness, but the little happiness of drinks, kisses and a good little car." But once we have set out on pilgrimage, once our passion has been awakened, "the little ways" won't do anymore. The sudden burst of light in our lives illuminates all the dark corners of our souls, and we are forced to search for the bigger happiness, which is called joy. We are forced to ask big questions with our whole heart.

Robert Coles records the words of a factory worker for whom the world was changed by the burst of light from tragic events in his life.

> *Twice, just twice, have I stopped and thought to myself, "Who are you, mister, and what are you doing here, and what should you be doing besides what you've been told by your boss and your neighbors and everyone else?" It was after my father died. It was when my little boy fell sick and he had leukemia, they thought. And for a month we stared death in the face with him. And for a month I wasn't the same person, the same person I usually am. They decided he didn't have leukemia and he'd be all right—and I told my wife that I had never lived like that before—all the wondering about the world, all the questions I asked. I don't mean my questions were so good, and I know everyone asks questions sometimes. But I asked them—I asked them with my whole heart.*

Living in the light means staring death in the face as a daily part of the pilgrimage. If we do, we won't be the same person we usually are. We will live and love in the world differently, because the new light keeps the big question alive inside us. Our attention span is all too brief. The light fades, and we soon get back to sleep in the twilight world of everyday life.

The various candles illuminating our world show up our frail and terminal state. We do not see clearly, and we often mistake power for the truth as if the person with the loudest voice or the country with the most weapons is right. When the *Challenger* exploded we all looked around for someone to blame, and the subsequent investigation tracked down the human error and folly behind the tragedy. The unanswerable question, however, was, Where was God? I heard in my mind the mocking and bitter comment of an atheist friend from college days. When tragedy struck he would say, "I know there's a mind behind it all somewhere!" Where was God when the *Challenger* went up in a blaze of light? Where are the seven who died that day? Where are they now? The light from the *Challenger* did this much for us. It enabled us to ask big questions with our whole hearts. We know this much. Each one of us owes God a death. This particular candle revealed a terrible secret—that the world cannot go on without sacrifice. This secret permeates the depths of all human endeavor and activity. The world cannot go on without the rhythm of death and resurrection. Those who have a passion for pilgrimage take on that rhythm for themselves. They know that at the heart of things there is a Great Passion that renews and refines all things in its burning heat and blinding light. The cycle of death and resurrection goes on with or without our consent.

Death, particularly under tragic circumstances, focuses all of our anger and frustration at a life that doesn't work as it is supposed to work. We have enough reminders of our frailty without the terrible illumination tragedy brings.

The passionate pilgrim sees the world by means of a light that is so bright that it absorbs all the shadows cast by the candles around the world. That light of Christ reveals one simple truth: *we belong to God*. We want to belong to God, yet exposure to the divine God feels like death at first. Such exposure means the death of the old self, the burning up of old patterns of believing and behaving, the surrender of worn-out perceptions. A burst of light gives us a chance to grow up.

We see the sunburst of a tragedy like that of the *Challenger* in the greater light of the Passion of God revealed in Jesus Christ. This God takes on the helplessness of a baby! He bears our weakness and vulnerability. This fact is the most blinding light there is. God-in-Jesus in Mary's arms is the same God who surrenders himself to the arms of the cross. God takes on our flesh. This is the nature of the Passion. In Christ, two lights come together: the light of tragedy, of which the *Challenger* is an example, and the light of hope. Tragedy and hope meet in the blinding collision of the cross.

The baby who nestled in Mary's arms holds the world in being. When I think of the light of God's Passion, I can dare ask the terrible question, Where is God when tragedy strikes? Seven were burned up in the *Challenger*. If God was anywhere, he was there in the flesh of those who died. And where are they who died? I hear the voice of God passionately respond, "They are with me!" The message is comforting, but is it true? And if it is true, why did their "homecoming" have to be like that? I was horrified to hear some glib believers refer to the end of the world in a nuclear holocaust as a wonderful way to go! Careless and shallow thinking about death and suffering puts everyone in danger.

When we ask for light, we may be getting more than we bargained for. You cannot look directly at the noonday sun without being dazzled and temporarily blinded. I am puzzled why people imagine that they can look God straight in the eye. The Judeo-Christian tradition insists that "no one can see God and live." Looking directly into the light of Truth brings either death or madness. To ask for light is extremely dangerous. What we might see when we look into the heart of things might be so terrifying that our first desire would be to tear our eyes out. To be enlightened, to be full of light, means that there is no place in us left unexposed. Who would want that? Who would not prefer the half-light? We would rather live in the twilight world of our "vital lies" than enter the dazzling darkness of God.

Light, then, does not always come to us as a blessing. It brings with it fresh challenges and responsibilities. For one thing, new light shows up our former blindness. When we feel "in the dark" we seek the light in dangerous and destructive places. In an unstable world, we may be tempted to embrace an enveloping darkness posing as the true light. The more enveloping the darkness, the more unwilling we are to give up the belief that we are truly in the light.

Our longing for enlightenment is one of the most dangerous passions of all. We can easily find ourselves imprisoned in the darkness of ideology or religious fanaticism. Doris Lessing wrote of the deadly darkness of ideology of her youth:

> *When I came to England, I found the Left could mean dull persons shouting at meetings, boring me to death with their egos. With words. Verbiage the more outrageous the less it meant. They hated art. In time, I came to fear that they hated people as well. Living lives of frenzied emotionality based on the sufferings of other persons in other countries about whom they seemed to care very little except to find them convenient for certain neurotic needs of their own.*[2]

Ideology is a fixed picture of reality that tells us where we belong and how things are supposed to be. What if the picture we have of reality was bought at great personal cost? The nagging feeling that it might be a fake, that we had given our lives in the service of an illusion, would drive us either into madness or into an even more rigid dogmatism. Pilgrims on this particular journey must always be prepared to find out that they are in the wrong. They must entertain the idea all the time, so that they are constantly available to greater light. Ideology is a kind of darkness that we embrace when things get out of hand and we don't know where to turn.

The alternative is not the darkness of indecisiveness. It is to be part of a continually self-correcting and self-donating community at the heart of which is wonder and worship. One cannot help but sympathize with many young people who, "having suffered the

chaos of parental indecisiveness during childhood, turn to fundamentalism with relief, sensing it in a compensation for the missing
link in their development."[3]

If fundamentalism is a problem in our culture, then so is its
extreme opposite—an unreflective "openness." This is another
kind of darkness. It is the belief that intolerance is more dangerous
than error. Robert Bellah and his colleagues who wrote *Habits of
the Heart* encountered a young woman whom they called Sheila
Larson. She had made up her own religion and named it
"Sheilaism" after herself. Bellah comments, "That suggests the possibility of over 220 million religions, one for each of us." In a
Gallup Poll a few years ago, 80 percent of Americans affirmed their
belief that "an individual should arrive at his or her own religious
beliefs independent of any churches or synagogues."[4] This is a
common and deeply entrenched belief in our culture. It is a darkness difficult to penetrate, because it looks attractive and plausible.
Do-it-yourself religion sounds wonderful. We make it up as we go
along without the hassle of history or tradition. If we do that, there
is no way we can test our beliefs. There is no way for us to be
grounded.

We are, then, faced with two kinds of darkness. There is the
darkness of a rigid, narrow-minded religiosity and a deeper darkness of a rootless, boundary-free openness that is, in the end,
alienating and destructive. Bellah writes:

> *To dissolve all boundaries, to relativize all moral judgments,
> would not only threaten the survival of the traditional reli-
> gious communities, it would also lead to a society in which
> no one would really want to live... There is a fear in our
> loose-bounded culture that strong belief in anything, partic-
> ularly in the area of right and wrong, means one wishes to
> coerce others into sharing one's views.*[5]

Allan Bloom also challenges the popular acceptance of loose-
boundedness. He derides the view that "there is no enemy other
than the man who is not open to everything." Openness to every-

thing means commitment to nothing. Bloom is quick to ask, "When there are no shared goals or vision for the public good, is the social contract any longer possible?"[6] Lost in the darkness of our own private worlds, we imagine that we are free. "God" becomes a mere sign for our own desires and wishes. But rootless and cut off from a life-bearing tradition, I don't know what or how to choose between conflicting desires. If everything carries equal weight, then nothing is important.

> God is the Iz-ness of the Is,
> The One-ness of our Cosmic Biz,
> The high, the low, the near, the far,
> The atom and evening star;
> The lark, the shark, the cloud, the clod,
> The whole darned Universe—that's God![7]

The sentiment expressed in the poem simply is not true. There is a world of glorious difference between the Creator and the creature. The light from the universe, from the isness of things, points beyond itself. Every creature sings with joy and delight, "I am not God! I am not the One you seek!" St. Augustine has the sea and the mountains sing out, "We are not God!" "Who then is God?" And the creatures reply, "It is he who made us!"

The questions are, Where is the true light, and How do we discern it? How do we know that we are not pursuing false lights and going even more deeper into darkness? We long for revelation. We long for clarity. We long for a bearer of the light to tell us who and where we are. If we are not awake and alert, we are ripe for the seductive words of Lucifer (the light-bearer). The writer of the Letter to the Ephesians warns his readers, "Once you were darkness, but now you are light in the Lord; walk as children of light.... Therefore it is said, 'Awake, O sleeper, and arise from the dead, and Christ shall give you light'" (Eph. 5:8, 14, RSV). Enlightenment, then, means being awake and being available to the power of new life in Christ. The gospel is an invitation to see the dazzling darkness of God concentrated in a wonderful particular, Jesus Christ.

The Light shines from a little baby in a manger. We see it shining, powerfully focused on a broken and ruined man on a cross. Ours is a very different vision from that of do-it-yourself religion. The God who was and is in Christ is focused and particular. He isn't the undifferentiated blob making up "everything" but the One in whom everything is held in being.

We need to be clear about the consequences of our believing, however vague and casual. The light by which we live, whether it be true or false, affects the world around us. Take, for example, the opportunist cults and the spirit-guide industry. There is a kind of franchise in spiritual junk food for those who want a do-it-yourself, no-fault religion. There may well be some truth in channeling. I don't know. I am more concerned with the messages and their implication for human behavior than with the messengers or channels themselves. There is Ramtha or the Ram who is a spirit guide for a very fashionable channeler. He is said to be a 35,000-year-old warrior. The "god" of which he speaks

> *is neither good or bad. God is entirely without morals and unjudgmental. There are no divine decrees. Isness is his only business—there is no such thing as evil. Nothing you can do, not even murder is wrong. There is no forgiveness of sins because there are no sins to forgive.*[8]

Ramtha, through his channel, says, "Every vile and wicked thing you do broadens your understanding." There is, of course, some light here. But the Ram goes on, "If you want to do any one thing, regardless of what it is, it would not be wise to go against that feeling; for there is an experience awaiting you and a grand adventure that will make your life sweeter." Who could resist that? It is the word *regardless* that plunges us into a maddening darkness. "Suppose a man feels the need to rape and kill a child... Murder is not a sin to be expiated, it is a teaching experience. You never have to *pay* for anything." This is the kind of "enlightenment" that plunges us into the darkness furthest away from our true home with one another in God. Not to be able to discern the difference between good and evil is to be in deep darkness. To affirm that there is no difference at all is to have slipped our human and humane moorings.

> *It is hardly surprising that the Ram has nothing to say about the poor and suffering… Everyone… whether he is starving or crippled… has chosen his experience for the purpose of gaining from it… simply leave [the masses] alone and allow them to evolve according to their own needs and designs.*[9]

To be full of light in our culture involves a secure income and a place to live. This false illumination has personal, social, and political implications. It neatly justifies our indifference and selfishness. "If a child is starving because of bad karma… or because its soul has chosen starvation as a teaching experience, why interfere?"

The light of doctrine makes a difference. The view that all people in the world—the street people, the mentally ill, the hungry—have *chosen* their fate is pernicious. It undermines our sense of connection with each other. It erodes our already faltering social contract. To live in a world without mutuality, responsibility, and compassion is to live in an inhuman world. What kind of human beings do we want to be? What happens to us when we lose all sense of right and wrong, when the thread of connection with others is severed? In the name of light and freedom, we are abandoned in an isolating craziness. A life that is accountable to nothing and no one is not worth living.

What, then does it mean to be truly "in the light"? How do we know whether we stand within its beams? What is demanded of us is obedience to an inner light. This obedience has a name. It is called "purity of heart," and purity of heart is to will one thing, to have a single eye. To have a pure heart means to know who we are and to know where we are going. This means giving up our individualist view of religion. It means continually questioning our own private judgments. There are three simple tests to see whether we are in the light or not. First, to be in the light is to move towards each other in pilgrimage. Second, to be in the light is to know the difference between ourselves and God. Third, to be in the light is to know that our choices matter and to accept responsibility for what we do. The light, whatever else it is, is for us to *see* each other. To be in the light is to begin to be formed into God's People. The Church is for pilgrims of the light who help each other tell the difference between restrictive fantasies and truly liberating flights of imagination.

In this pilgrimage home, we move toward each other. That is what the light is for. As we move toward each other, we are made into something new. We are made into a people for the transforming of the world.

The rabbis tell a wonderful story about a teacher who asks his students about the dawning of true light. "When can you tell when day is breaking?" One student suggests that it is when you look down the road and you see an animal and there is enough light to tell whether it is a fox or a dog. "No," insists the rabbi, "that's not the right answer." Another student ventures to answer the question. "It's when you look at an orchard and you can tell the difference between an apple and a pear tree." The rabbi shakes his head, and the students, in frustration, all shout, "Then, tell us! When can you tell when the day has dawned?" The rabbi replies, "Day breaks when you look at a man or a woman and know that he or she is your brother or your sister. Until you can do that, no matter what time of day it is, it is always night."

The true light for pilgrims is simply tested in this way. "To love and to reconcile and to forgive—only this matters." This is what it is to *see*.

Study Questions

1. Jones writes of sometimes feeling trapped and in the dark, resistant to being awakened to the search for joy, the bigger happiness. In what areas of you life are you in the dark? What prompts your movements towards love, reconciliation, and forgiveness?

2. Jones states, "When we put ourselves at the center the light goes out" (p. 54). How does this assertion relate to the call to be self-correcting and self-donating? What tensions are strung between these poles of self-awareness?

3. "To be enlightened," Jones writes, "to be full of light, means that there is no place in us left unexposed. Who would want that?" (p. 57). What reasons can you offer for seeking this dangerous experience that feels at first like death? What makes the risk worth taking?

4. Jones names fundamentalism and unreflective "openness" as two extremely opposite problems in our culture (p. 59). What are the hazards of each of these tendencies? What can help us balance between "a rigid, narrow-minded religiosity" and "a rootless, boundary-free openness"?

5. What are the three simple tests Jones suggests to see whether we are in the light? (See pp. 62–63.) What happens when we are in the light? Why?

5.
A HEART WILLING TO GIVE ITSELF AWAY

"To love and to reconcile and to forgive—only this matters." But how are we to do this? As we go deeper into the journey, the agenda gets tougher. Unless we are committed to a life of spiritual unconsciousness, there is no way to go through life without our eventually asking some big questions. One of the illusions that we entertain from time to time is that there will be an exception made in our case and that we shall live forever. There are numerous stories and legends about people looking for the secret of immortality, for the drinkable gold, the elixir of life.

There are two reasons for our desire to cheat death. The first is our understandable longing to make sense, not only of our own pain, but the pain of the world. What are we to make of "the still sad music of humanity"? The second reason has to do with our capacity for joy and wonder. We find it inconceivable that we could be cut off from such moments forever. Even if we are deprived of them at the moment, we dream of their return. Experiences of pain and wonder push us into probing the mystery of death.

Experiences of pain can make some of us long for death. The euphemism for the death of someone in pain, when I was growing up, was "a happy release." In many cases this is an apt description. Pain can also push us over the edge into despair. Maybe it is all pointless after all? Wonder is the antidote to despair. When pain and wonder are experienced together, a secret begins to emerge with regard to the possible significance of our lives. The secret is very simple: living means giving. True living requires surrender. If we really want to live, we have to find some means of giving ourselves away. We have a choice in the face of wonder and of pain. We can repress the secret of surrender and live a life that is marked and marred by a rhythm of self-justification, or we can go on the pilgrimage of sacrifice and surrender. We can wall up the heart, or we can give it away.

There is, however, a third way that is neither self-justifying (at least not in the pharisaical sense) nor sacrificial. The way of the "happy pagan" (a way which I find very attractive) is one that is often exuberant, vital, and inventive. In the pagan view of things, everything is, in principle, fixable. With money and know-how, there is no such thing as an unfixable situation. There is, however, an underbelly to paganism in our society—a rootlessness and weightlessness that rob its adherents of the grounds for hope. Our pagan society is an addictive society. We are addicted to security, to power, to substances and sex, to ideas, and to money. Spiritual maturity is a process of withdrawal from whatever dulls our pain and erodes our capacity for wonder. Listening to the pain of the world and responding in joy and wonder to its marvels are required of those who would enter the mystery of the Passion.

When I am willing to listen and respond I find that I need all the support I can muster. I need your help. I need your help not only to bear and interpret the pain but also to teach me how to enjoy the world. I do not know how. Over the years in the healing experience of talking with fellow pilgrims, I hear a great deal about pain and wonder. What is lacking, however, is a story to bind it all together. We lack a Passion Play. Many of us don't know how to interpret the world and, therefore, we don't know how to enjoy it. We have no life-bearing tradition or story by which we can understand our own drama. We have no way of celebrating what we know.

The secret shines through, if only we could see it. Living means giving. Resurrection is always preceded by crucifixion. It is the law of life. This secret is to be trusted and celebrated. If you want to live, give.

We are made after the image of the God who gives himself away. The mystery of that self-giving is what Easter is all about. The closer we get to our destination the closer we are to the crucifixion. Holy Week and Easter are not only times when we remember God's Passion for us. They also invite us into our own passion. Lent is a long period of reality-testing that questions our view of ourselves and our world. As we have seen, the process of testing is for the purpose of making new space inside us. Through it, our lives have been given new direction and purpose. We have had to face the truth about our sinning, and we have learned the hard lesson of accepting responsibility for who we are and what we do. We have had to acknowledge our capacity for and our connivance with evil. We have been challenged to embrace a "certain kind of suffering." There has been a movement toward "home." We have found that our dead ends can be God's way of opening up new avenues of exploration. There is, however, no way round the last extremity, which is death itself.

It seems that in matters of life and death the very best and the very worst come out in us. Sometimes, in the face of a common danger, there is a renewed sense of solidarity among us. We band together and support each other. We find inner resources of which we had little inkling before the crisis that bound us together. I grew up in England with stories of the quiet heroism of Londoners who cared for each other during the terrible days of the Second World War when the city was the target of enemy bombers. Friends died daily, and people lived one day at a time, facing death *together*.

At other times a common danger can cut us off from each other. As we have seen, we try to exile people to the last place on earth. Others become our enemies, and sometimes mere exile won't do. In our darkest selves, we wish that they would cease to exist. This is particularly true of those who suffer from deadly illnesses. A sickness for which there is no known cure is not only tragic for the victims, it has the power to capture the imagination of those who have not contracted the disease. We often see illness as a kind of divine punishment. No matter how irrational this is, the idea runs very deep in many of us. When we are afflicted we find ourselves saying to ourselves, What have I done to deserve this?

In the nineteenth century the "fashionable" and dreaded disease was tuberculosis. It was called consumption and was easily romanticized in such operas as *La Bohème* and *La Traviata*. A Victorian heroine was almost required to be consumptive. In our century (at least until recently) the disease that most captured our imaginations was cancer. Cancer was *the* disease. I remember hearing of the death in the family, and an aunt asked, "What did she die of? It wasn't cancer, was it?" To her relief the answer was no. She said, with considerable relief, "Thank God!" Dying is bad enough, but, in our culture, it matters what you die of. It is important that we die of something respectable and acceptable.

In these last few years of the twentieth century *the* disease is AIDS. The tragedy of AIDS is a prism through which we can examine many of the problems and tragedies of modern society. AIDS is not a "proper" thing to die of. *"Die, but for God's sake, don't die of AIDS!"* The word itself is frightening. Notions of illness and punishment are found together in the depths of the human pysche. Add to that already explosive mix our sexuality and the destructive potential is incalculable. Sickness, like sexuality, always raises questions of human identity. In our most intimate moments as well as in moments of extreme vulnerability and frailty, we ask, who am I? What has happened to me? Who am I now? When we are confronted with someone who is dying, the unasked questions are often, Who is she? Who is he? Where is my son? Where is my daughter? Most terrible of all is our attitude toward those we do not know. Those whom we would reject and condemn, we first rob of their identity. In their case the horrifying question is not, Who are they? But *Why* are they? How dare they *be*! How dare they continue to exist. Die of AIDS if you must, but die quickly, die anonymously, die alone, but for God's sake die!

Certain kinds of illnesses capture the vindictive spirit that lurks in all of us. AIDS is such a sickness. When I give in to that spirit, I come to believe that the preservation of my identity requires the diminishment of yours. I feel safe if others are condemned, isolated, and quarantined.

For all of us, the stark reality of death raises the fundamental question of human identity. We pilgrims of the Spirit know that we share a common identity with all our brothers and sisters. Baptism is a sacrament that celebrates and signifies this new mutuality. It is the entrance into the mystery and terror of a shared identity. As pilgrims journeying with passion into the Passion of

God, we have no identity that we possess in our own right. Your identity isn't exclusively yours anymore. It is ours. If we are to be healed, each of us has to come to the terrifying conclusion that we are no one and nowhere without each other.

There is a Latin-American baptismal liturgy in which the priest takes the one to be baptized and plunges that person into the water and says, "I kill you, in the name of the Father and of the Son and of the Holy Spirit! And I raise you up to a new life in Christ!" Being a pilgrim on the journey home requires such a radical exchange. It is heart surgery. The heart of stone is exchanged for the heart of flesh. We are always being raised up into a wider and more inclusive fellowship.

Religious people easily find themselves in an ever-narrowing circle of exclusion. What is supposed to be the generous circle of God's love becomes the tight and narrow enclave of the chosen few. St. Augustine raged against this narrowness of vision when he tried to deal with the heretical Donatists in North Africa. "As Christ sits in glory at his right hand, the possessor of the whole world, these Donatists have the audacity to say to him, here is your kingdom! And instead of the whole world, they give him Africa!" Instead of the whole world with all the people in it we offer God the little "village" in which we live. Death is not only a great leveler, it is also a great bond. It makes us citizens of one world. Teilhard de Chardin wrote, "What I want to do is to express... the mixed feelings of pride, hope, disappointment, expectation of one who sees himself no longer as a Frenchman or a Chinaman, but as a *terrestrial*." We pilgrims are terrestrials who have been to the last place on earth and who are willing to enter into a solidarity with others that is as binding as death.

Our journey together to Calvary and Easter is a road away from addictive behavior, a passionate search for an identity that is both lost and wounded. The road to healing leads right to the foot of the cross and into the mystery of God's Passion and ours.

All that has gone before has been to prepare us for what is coming. We are en route to the Passion. The Palm Sunday liturgy plays it out for us in dramatic detail. It is then that we enter the great drama of Holy Week with its climax at the Three Great Days of Good Friday, Holy Saturday, and Easter Day. Lent prepares us for the drama that transforms our drifting into pilgrimage. Our journey began with a powerful image of the conflict between clock-time and dream-time. "The people of the dream watched the people of the clock come up out of the sea." Time forces us to face the consequences of our sinning, our capacity for evil, and the challenge of willed suffering. Time brings us to the final moment of our death. Each of us is in terminal state. "None of us is going to get out of this alive!" Death and the Clock go together.

In the Eastern tradition there is a critical period in our lives that is a privileged opportunity for spiritual growth. This time is called the period "between dreams." Dreaming is essential for our existence. It holds life together by series of images and pictures. We need to dream if life is to be worth living. From time to time, however, something wakes us up. Much to our consternation we find ourselves in a deep and impenetrable darkness. There is no light, no dream to hold life together. The bottom falls out of everything. In our panic we try to go back to sleep to recapture the old dream. The spiritual masters suggest that this moment of panic is a thing to hold onto and treasure. The time "between dreams" is a place to stay and wait in the darkness so that a new and larger dream has the chance to emerge. It is only in the waiting that the horizons of our dreaming can explode and expand. The new dream will make new space for us and send our lives in a new direction.

The questions for today are, How far do you sense that the drama is being played out in you? How far are you willing to wait "between dreams" to allow a new world to emerge for you? How far are you prepared to wake up? How far are you available to the possibility? The truth is that the gospel promise of new life is available to us insofar as we are willing to enter our own passion story. The season of Lent and Easter is a time when God's Passion for us and our passion for God collide and make something new.

Keri Hulme, a New Zealand author, in her novel *The Bone People*, writes:

They were nothing more than people, by themselves. Even paired, any pairing, they would have been nothing more than people by themselves. But all together, they have become the heart and muscles and mind of something perilous and new, something strange and growing and great. Together, all together, they are the instruments of change.[1]

This is a brilliant description of what God is doing with us as a people. In a time of passion we are made into "something perilous and new" so that we may "together, all together" become "instruments of change" in the world.

It is not accidental that bread and wine are central to our understanding of Passion. They are symbols of transformation. Think what grapes have to go through to become wine. We are God's grapes being turned into wine for the sake of the world. Grapes, however are also signs in Scripture of the wrath of God, which is the dark transforming side of the kind of love that will never let us be less than we are meant to be. The grapes of wrath are turned into the wine of celebration. The "anger" of God is turned into joy and delight in God's people.

Death has to be faced in a world often largely indifferent to us. Perhaps life isn't worth living anyway. Is there anything worth dying for? One of the dangers of the reductionist view many people have of modern science is that our own insignificance is so serious that nothing that we do or are matters. Modern science suggests that the universe is indeterminate. Chance plays a large part in events. For some people this is reason to despair. I believe in the God of Chance! Chance in the universe means that the story isn't over. The drama hasn't yet played itself out. Everything is not cut and dried. As one scientist puts it,

the reality of chance is not merely compatible with an understanding of creation, but required by it. This strong assertion is based on the claim that only in a world with real uncertainty can people grow into free and responsible children of a loving [God].[2]

What is peddled by popular religion is not uncertainty (which is part of faith) but rigid certainty in the name of faith. Most of us prefer certainty. If we are to enter the mystery of faith, we have to wake up to uncertainty (the place "between dreams"), which is a kind of dying.

The resonant imagery of the valley of dry bones (in Ezekiel 37) comes to mind. The prophet looks over the valley of death and asks the question, Can these bones live? The valley of dry bones is a powerful metaphor for where we find ourselves today. We are at the point in the story where only the miracle of grace can rescue us from our dryness. Only the breath of God can make these bones live. We, like Abraham and Sarah, are as good as dead. But listen to the rattle of the bones as they begin to connect when they are breathed on once more. Listen to them and us being made into "something perilous and new."

Let us look for a moment at our own dry bones, our grave clothes. Let us see what is killing us, holding us back, eating away at us from the inside. What exactly is our status in the world? From the popular but inaccurate view some have of modern science we are animals with no hope. Many scientists, of course, do not believe this. Being an animal doesn't worry me. In fact I rejoice in it, but I do not agree with a Stephen Jay Gould, for example, who says, "A crab is not lower nor less complex than a human being in any meaningful way." I know of no crab that has written a symphony. Nor do I know of any crustacean libraries. While I am willing to see myself on one long continuum with crabs, distinctions are important. I acknowledge my solidarity with other animals. But it isn't true that I am not different in any meaningful way. By God, I am and so are you! For one thing we can eat crabs and kill each other. In some respects we may even be "lower" in that we kill our own species. But we are different from crabs and in a meaningful way. This pseudoscientific reductionism has led otherwise sane religious people to reject the teaching of evolution. There's a marvelous apocryphal comment attributed to the wife of the bishop of Gloucester in the 1860s. "Let us hope that evolution is not true, but if it is true, let us hope that it doesn't become common knowledge!" The notion is that, if we are at one with the monkeys and the crabs, there is no hope. Such mistaken reductionism is like a winding-sheet. We find ourselves wrapped in grave clothes, lying in a sepulcher of the spirit as good as dead. It is, of course, a wrong inference. The fact that God made us—humans, crabs, monkeys—in one long chain of being, makes the created order all the more wonderful. It is sad that many people believe that if evolution is true then they don't matter. It doesn't take much to deaden the soul.

Take, for example, the issue of women who carry to term a child for a couple who cannot have children. Some time ago there was a dispute over the "ownership" of a child who came to be known as baby M. Who are the parents of this child? The case raised the question of what human beings are by forcing us to face the issue of our "rentability." Is it possible for us to rent out wombs, sperm, and eggs to each other without dire consequences? And if it comes to be common practice, are we willing to take the consequences and count the cost?

What about you is rentable? Aren't our relationships descants on the sad tune of rentability? The principle of rentability provides the winding-sheet of many a relationship. We don't really give ourselves to each other. We rent ourselves out, because we do not know how to trust each other. I do not trust you, but I am willing to "rent" myself out to you for a suitable return. The idea that persons or parts of persons are rentable seems to me to be a dangerous kind of reductionism that contributes to the dryness of our bones. The stench of death is in our nostrils. Reductionism is what the wrath of God is all about. God's loving anger says to us, "I take you more seriously that you do yourselves!" When we take ourselves seriously in the way that God does, we experience the "wrath" and the celebration in one instant as grapes are transformed into wine. We are called to be more than what we now know of ourselves. Drunk with the wine of God's love, we find ourselves being made into "something perilous and new." We are not, after all, rentable commodities but people who are so secure that we are free to give ourselves away.

Wendell Berry's hero in his story *The Memory of Old Jack* bemoans our "modern ignorance."

The modern ignorance is in people's assumptions that they can outsmart their own nature. It is in the arrogance that will believe nothing that cannot be proved, and respect nothing it cannot understand, and value nothing it cannot sell.

Our homecoming, if it is anything, must be a return to ourselves. It involves believing things that cannot be proved, respecting things that pass our understanding, and realizing that what we are given is beyond price.

Our Lenten agenda is a daring journey of freedom that does not flinch from the fact that each one of us is a movement towards death. Death puts your whole existence into question. Death takes you by the scruff of the neck and says, "Hey! You! Yes, you! Wake up! What are you living for? Who are you living for?" Death is tough on us. How do we counter the argument that we Christian are in love with death and do not love this present life?

The truth is that we Christians are called to love the world afresh with a powerful, intimate, and life-bearing love of which those who protest against it are deeply ignorant. After all, the person who can give his or her love freely is the one who loves most intimately and loyally. Someone who tries to rent love out is not a lover. And only he or she can love freely who is not obliged to give.

The person of faith, the person who lives with uncertainty and chance (that is, one who has freely and in faith accepted death's inevitability), is one who is truly free to love the world. He or she who has not accepted death only exploits the world.[3]

The Lenten agenda—sin, guilt, suffering, and death—points to the hard road of freedom. God passionately loves us, not in order for us to wall up our hearts, but in order to free us to give them away to God, to each other, and to the world. That is what the drama of Palm Sunday and Holy Week is about. Grapes are crushed into wine. Walls surrounding our hearts are broken down so that we can give them away. The drama invites us to shed our grave clothes and live from a new place inside us.

The pattern is more familiar to us than we realize. It is commonplace for anyone who has tried to love. We all have experience of this first hand. In the story of the initiation of Lame Deer, a contemporary Native American, there is an important moment that illustrates the costliness of love. As preparation for going into the Dream Pit for three days, Lame Deer was given certain things by the medicine man to fortify him.

> *Besides the pipe, the medicine man had also given me a gourd. In it were forty small squares of flesh my grandmother cut from her arm with a razor blade. I had seen her do it. Blood had been streaming down from her shoulder to her elbow as she carefully put down each piece of skin on a handkerchief anxious not to lose a single one... Someone dear to me had undergone pain, given me something of herself, part of her body, to help me pray and make me strong-hearted. How could I be afraid with so many people—living and dead—praying for me?*

The same pattern of self-giving love is present here at the Eucharist. Someone loves you so much that he gives himself to you and for you so that you may be strong-hearted enough to give yourself away. At the altar, Sunday by Sunday, as we break the bread and share the wine, we participate in a great drama of love. St. Augustine wrote this, concerning the apostles:

> *They were of the poor who "ate and were satisfied," because they suffered the same things as they ate. He gave his supper. He gave his passion. You will be satisfied at his table insofar as you share his passion.* [paraphrase]

In the pilgrimage of Lent, we face death in the hope of the risen life. We find ourselves in a great company of wine-makers! We are the grapes pressed into wine for the world. What a dream this is! What an expansive and wonderful dream for the healing of the world. You and I are invited into a great drama of transformation, so that, together, we might be made into "something perilous and new."

Lady Julian of Norwich, the fourteenth-century mystic, was given a terrible and glorious vision of Christ's Passion. Years later, she reflected on its meaning. She wrote:

From time to time these things were revealed I had often wanted to know what was our Lord's meaning. It was more than fifteen years after that I was answered in my spirit's understanding. You would know our Lord's meaning in this thing? Know it well.

Love was his meaning.
Who showed it you? Love.
What did he show you? Love.
Why did he show it? For love.

Hold on to this and you will know and understand love more and more. But you will not know or learn anything else—ever.

This is our dream: the dream of a heart—not walled up—but willing to give itself away. If feels like death, but it is the way to fullness of life. This is paradox of transformation. To live is to give away your heart. To love is to give yourself away.

Study Questions

1. Jones puts forth two reasons for our desire to cheat death, hoping for an exception to be made in our case that will allow us to live forever. What are they? Name ways in which these reasons have been played out in your own life.

2. "Spiritual maturity," Jones writes, "is a process of withdrawal from whatever dulls our pain and erodes our capacity for wonder" (p. 66). What lessons of spiritual maturity have you been given in your lifetime? What helps you to bear the burden of listening to the pain of the world?

3. Reread the story of the Valley of Dry Bones in Ezekiel 37. Ezekiel's listening to the pain of the world brought him to the question, "Can these bones live?" How are we today dried out and in need of the miracle of grace that the breath of God brings? What voices are prophesying to our dry bones?

4. Jones suggests that we wrap ourselves in a winding-sheet, the grave clothes that hold us back from truly giving ourselves to one another, rather than wondering in the connectedness of creation (p. 73). What experiences in your past have helped you to trust others, to free yourself for self-giving? What experiences have taught you to follow more closely "the sad tune of rentability" that separates you from relationships?

II.
THE WEEK OF CRUCIFIXION

6.
God Has Fallen in Love with You and Wants You to Come Home

To love is to give yourself away. You can dare throw yourself into the pilgrimage, because God has fallen in love with you so much that he has sent his son into the world to bring you home. This is the basic message of Christianity. Twenty-five years ago one of my mentors told me that the truth that I was loved all the way through was "the brute fact of the universe." I am now just coming to believe it. Christianity is a love affair beginning with the gasp of astonishment with which all love affairs begin. Christianity is the School of Love. It is a hard school in which there are battles of life and death. It is the only school that matters.

Christianity, then, is an invitation to fall in love, an invitation to come home. It reminds me of the classic, if hackneyed, line in the play or the movie: "Come home, all is forgiven!" It is strange that our longing for love makes us feel uneasy—not at home. It is even stranger that our aching and our longing lead us away from the true object of our desire. Our longing has a double edge to it. It gives us an intimation of what we long for and yet also shows us how far we have wandered from the path that leads to it. It is not unlike the experience of being on the "wrong" train or the "wrong" bus. We thought we knew where we were going, only we find that we're being taken further and further away from our desired destination. Dead ends serve a purpose. They bring us up against our desires and our inability to satisfy them. They bring us to ourselves. Walker Percy's hero in *The Thanatos Syndrome* says to himself,

> *I discovered that it is not sex that terrifies people. It is that they are stuck with themselves. They are frightened out of their wits that they are not doing what, according to experts, books, films, TV, they are supposed to be doing.*[1]

We are stuck with ourselves, and we rarely like what we're stuck with. If we are fortunate enough to have learned the hard lesson of proper self-love, we still feel that we are not yet "home." A middle-aged friend of mine was driving on the highway recently and found himself spontaneously saying to himself over and over again, "I want to go home. I want to go home!" The point is that we are lost. We find ourselves at the last place on earth. We have wandered far from ourselves, and the Christian story of the Fall is our way of trying to understand how we got lost. The Fall is a way of speaking about our sense of "not being at home." This sense of lostness seems to be built in. Restlessness is in our blood. As the theologian Karl Rahner put it, a human being is "the question for which there is no answer."

How, then, do we respond to our not being "at home"? Passion for pilgrimage leads us into the mystery of lostness from which we learn a new way of loving. This is what the season of Lent is all about. Its climax is Holy Week, which is the most solemn and momentous time in the Church's Year, when the love affair is revealed in all its wonder and glory. Its message is clear and simple: God has fallen in love with you and wants you to come home. We find ourselves in the middle of a love affair that is leading to a strange and terrible climax called the Crucifixion. We have an appointment with our Lover on Good Friday. It is a tryst we would rather not keep.

The kind of loving that leads to Good Friday seems crazy, foolish, and even irresponsible. Jesus turns my idea of loving upside down. On the night before the Passion, Jesus sends out his betrayer, Judas: "Go and do what you have to do and do it quickly!" Jesus then claims that he has been glorified (John 13:31) and says, "A new commandment I give to you, that you love one another *even as I have loved you.*" We are to love one another with that kind of love. My immediate response is to say, "No, thank you! This is not what I had in mind. This is a journey for which I am unprepared." The words *even as I have loved you* fill me with dread. God loves us passionately and invites our passionate response. I am not sure that I can stand God's being in love with me. I would rather stay where I am than have to find my way home by a road that leads to Calvary.

The road home passes through a Passion. It is a heartbreaking pilgrimage, yet without the heartbreak that passion brings. I begin to die of terminal boredom—boredom because nothing is *moving* inside me. The human heart seems destined to burst, either with longing and gratitude or with anger and disappointment. This is a time for the bursting of hearts. What a terrible love is offered us in Jesus Christ! The contradictions are enormous. They crush us. The clash of opposites breaking the heart of God echo in our own depths. If we dare listen to them, they will break our hearts also.

The week begins with Palm Sunday, the theme of which is the kingship of Christ. We long for a king, a ruler, a president. We want desperately for someone to be in charge. If only someone would take the world by the scruff of the neck and rule it with clarity and strength. We can feel this longing for someone to be in charge in the pervasive and freewheeling frustration, disappointment, and anger in national and world politics. When bankruptcy of the political process is revealed and our own political irresponsibility stares us in the face, there is an aching void in our common life. We long for a "king." There are many of us who, given a push, might admit our longing for a dictator (a benign one, of course) who would take away the ambiguity and the struggle and help the world through the agency of the United States "to shape up" and get moving. When we feel leaderless, we turn nasty. We become vindictive. We become mean-spirited. Someone has to pay. Why doesn't God do something? All God appears to "do" is, in Jesus, to betray himself into our hands. Like the crowds two thousand years ago, we can yell "Crucify him! Crucify him!" as easily as "Hosanna to the Son of David!" In these two shouts is heard the clashing of contradictions in the Passion Story. Holy Week intensifies the contradictions, as we come to realize that we have in Jesus a useless and broken leader. There wells up in us a voice that dares to say, "Given the world as it is, God has a lot to answer for!"

The message of Holy Week is that God *does* answer for it in Jesus on the cross. God is a ruler who is manifested in brokenness and weakness. God is the king who breaks our hearts so that they may be enlarged. The contradictory feelings inside us play out the drama: the longing, the gratitude, the disappointment, the aching, the anger—all erupt within us. This is the Passion. This is passion. It is ours and it is God's. It is ours together. God answers for it all in Jesus Christ.

Holy Week is a time for our hearts to burst, a time to trust our own inner experience of things, which tells us that in the breaking of the heart there is new life, new power, new energy. But I have no stomach for the cost. The gateway to life and the road to love is through God's Passion. No wonder we resist it. No wonder we domesticate the cross and try to trivialize its impact. Yet I continue to be fascinated by the love revealed here. I am drawn to it even as I am repelled by it. There is a kind of passion—even a kind of pain—for which we are starved. Unless we can get back in touch with that passion and that pain, we are already as good as dead. The reason is simple. God is at the heart of this passion and pain, and where God is there is life in all its fullness. That is why all but the hardest of hearts are moved by the Passion Story. It strikes chords deep within us and plays a music too deep for words.

Anthony Bloom, the Russian Orthodox archbishop in London, once observed, "Of course the Christian God exists. He is so absurd, no one could have invented him!" There is an important truth here. If you were to invent a God, you could do a lot better than the broken God of Calvary. Jesus reveals a God who is a victim. What kind of a God is that? In Jesus, we see a God who is vulnerable, a God who betrays himself into our hands. God is at our mercy. What is the use of a God like that? To add insult to injury, the Christian tradition claims that we are made in the image of this weak and vulnerable deity!

You belong to this God. Many a time you have fancied a deity of your own devising. You have even thought of yourself in the role of God. Well, now is your chance. Your moment is coming. If you want to know what God is like, look at Jesus. If you want to be like God, be like Jesus.

Holy Week, then, presents us with a question. What would it

be like to obey a God who reveals himself as self-giving love? We know something of this kind of love, which steps aside to allow others to *be*, in our everyday experience. The poet C. Day Lewis wrote these words about his son growing up. The scene is a sporting event at the boy's school during which the son turns from his father and goes off with his friends.

I have had worse partings, but none that so
Gnaws my mind still. Perhaps it is roughly
Saying what God alone could perfectly show—
How self-hood begins with walking away,
And love is proved in the letting go.

Love is proved in the letting go! What kind of music plays in your heart when you learn that part of loving is knowing when to allow another to walk away? What kind of God reveals himself to us in such vulnerability? When we wait at the foot of the cross, we learn that love has as much to do with letting go as with holding on. Anyone who has tried to love knows this from the inside. Anyone who has tried to love has caught a glimpse of what God is like. All our hurts and failures to love, all our moments of passion, show us the broken heart of God.

We know what real love is about, yet we resist what we know. We resist it not because it is hard to understand but because the heartbreaking drama of love wants to play itself out in us. The drama of love is not something "out there." It is in our blood. Whenever we try to love, we enter the mystery of God, whether we believe in him or not. Whenever we try to love, we find the cross. The way of love is cruciform, because love, to be true and free, must always carry within it the possibility of rejection. Our God, in Jesus Christ, always reveals himself to us in a form that we can reject. The cross bullies no one, coerces no one.

Holy Week is a homecoming to ourselves. It is coming home to one another. We dread it even as we ache for it. Our homecoming has something to do with what we believe about our final destination.

People often ask me about life after death. It is a central and important question and one that is both easy and difficult to answer: easy because I do believe in life after death; hard because I see my role as *not* answering questions. In fact, I believe that priests are not so much people with answers as ones who guard the important questions and keep them alive. The issue, for me, is not so much the question of life after death as a sort of hesitation before birth. My struggle with sin, evil, and suffering has something to do with the fact that I am unwilling to allow myself to be fully alive. Parts of me are left unborn and uncared for. Of course, I walk the streets as if I am fully alive. In reality, I am often "dead in my tracks." Rather than make my way home to myself, to others, and to God, I opt for deadly compromises with my friends. I choose to love them only a little bit. I like to keep lots of me in reserve, just in case. In case of what? I don't know. I hold myself back and get exhausted and cheat myself and others. I try to go it alone because no one is to be trusted. I do not trust myself. Why should I trust you? It seems more preferable and much easier to maintain a master-slave relationship to people and things, particularly if I can persuade myself that I am the master. In the process I find, of course, that I am the slave, and I find myself crying out, "What on earth has become of me?" William Golding, in his novel *Free Fall*, has his hero cry out, "[What is] the connection between the little boy, clear as spring water, and the man like a stagnant pool?…Oh, the continent of a man, the peninsulas, capes, deep bays and high hills. How shall I be rid of this kingdom, how shall I give it away?"

I don't know how to trust in such a way that I can give myself away, and I'm not sure that I want to. I know that I will do almost anything to avoid the three things required of me if I am to find my way home. I have to learn to accept three things that frighten and repel me: tragedy, suffering, and failure.

In the novel, *The Sinner of St. Ambrose*, the author puts these words into the mouth of a Roman official:

Our whole age, our whole Roman world, had gone dead in its heart because it feared tragedy, took flight from suffering and abhorred failure. In fear of tragedy we worshipped power. In fear of suffering we worshipped security. In fear of failure we worshipped success. Yea, in fear of the intensity of life there is in tragedy, we worshipped the coldness of death there is in power. In dread of the fertile growth there is in suffering we worshipped the sterile obediences of security. In terror of the healing love there is in failure we worshipped the corrupt denial of one another there is in success. During the rising splendor of our thousand years we had grown cruel, practical and sterile. We did win the whole world. We did lose our own souls.

Insofar as I avoid tragedy, suffering, and failure as important parts of human experience, I cut myself off from my homecoming. I have a Judas inside me who will not let go. I get trapped inside myself, in that hell that is me and me alone. All I am left with is my own sweating self. The only taste I have in my mouth is *me*. Christ, in his Passion, offers me a way out of the maze that is "me." It means my being willing to put my hand in yours and your putting yours in mine so that *together* we might find our way home.

Holy Week culminates in a great conflict of love and trust that is played out in the heart of God. Holy Week is the Great Journey out of our private hells into the homecoming of new possibilities. Insofar as I am willing to enter into the mystery of this week, especially the Great Three Days at its end, I will learn what it is to love. Good Friday, Holy Saturday, and Easter Day are all parts of one single event. They are expressions of God's love calling us home.

Easter enables me to remember my longing for home. Remembering is hard because there is always pain as well as joy in the process. Yet even if my memories are painful they have no power to destroy me, because the cross of Christ tells me that there is nothing I have done, nothing I am, that is worthy of hatred or abandonment. We are loved, and God aches for us to come home. And there is no better place to do it than at the altar when the Eucharist is celebrated. In the sign of the broken bread we see that love, like bread, is nothing until it is broken and given away. The hard and wonderful lesson of love is that we are nothing until we can give ourselves away to each other, to the world, and to God. The miracle is that God is only God in the breaking and the giving away. The secret of loving is in the bread broken. In Holy Week we discover the secret of this bread. Think of what goes into the baking of a loaf of bread, from the grinding of the wheat to the waiting for the dough to rise, from the working of the yeast to the fire of the oven. It is not accidental that the breaking and eating of bread is the central act of Christian worship. It is also central to our self-understanding. Our souls have to wait in darkness for their own rising and submit to the burning heat of transformation. We are invited to submit to a process of healing and forgiveness so that we can be truly at home with ourselves, with each other, and with God.

STUDY QUESTIONS

1. Jones was told "that the truth that I was loved all the way through was 'the brute fact of the universe.'" Christianity, he says, "is an invitation to fall in love…" What does our culture say about falling in love? What have been your experiences of falling in love? How is it for you to imagine God doing so?

2. "God has fallen in love with you and wants you to come home" (p. 81). How does this "crazy, foolish, even irresponsible" love reveal itself? What does it suggest to you about your own loving? Was this what you had in mind? "What would it be like to obey a God who reveals himself as self-giving love?"

3. "Love is proved in the letting go! What kind of music plays in your heart when you learn that part of loving is knowing when to allow another to walk away?" (p. 84). How do you respond?

4. On pages 82–83, Jones states, "God is a ruler who is manifested in brokenness and weakness." He writes of dreading homecoming even as we ache for it (p. 84). Where in your life are brokenness and weakness manifested? Who or what helps you to guard the important questions of those areas and keep them alive? What do you make of Jones's comment that "love, like bread, is nothing until it is broken and given away"?

7.
HOMECOMING—FACING WHAT WE DREAD

The Sunday before Lent in the Orthodox Church is called the Sunday of Forgiveness. This sets the tone of the Great Fast of Lent. Tradition insists that a fast without mutual love would be a fast of demons. Three simple words sum up the spirit of our pilgrimage: Love one another. Lent is the time when the stark simplicity of these words comes home to us. We are called to love one another to the end, and without exceptions. Unless love is to the end and openhearted to all, it is not love at all but a destructive force.

St. Basil the Great wrote:

> *Do not limit the benefit of fasting merely to abstinence from food, for a true fast means refraining from evil. Loose every unjust bond, put away your resentment against your neighbor, forgive him his offences. Do not let your fasting lead only to wrangling and strife. You do not eat meat, but you devour your brother/your sister; you abstain from wine, but not from insults. So all the labor of your fast is useless.*

These words set the tone for the whole Lenten season and put everything we do in the service of love. Fasting means refraining from evil. If we are to be instruments in God's hands against the forces of evil, we have to face our dread and our impotence in the face of it. Acknowledging our dread is a sound and firm step towards home.

In the spring of 1870, William James touched the rock bottom of depression—an experience of mindless terror.

> *Whilst in this state of philosophic pessimism and general depression of spirits about my prospects, I went one evening in a dressing-room in the twilight to procure some article that was there; when suddenly there fell upon me without warning, just*

as if it came out of the darkness, a horrible fear of my own existence. Simultaneously there arose in my mind the image of an epileptic patient whom I had seen in the asylum, a black-haired youth with a greenish skin, entirely idiotic, who used to sit all day on one of the benches, or rather shelves against the wall, with his knees drawn up against his chin, and the course grey undershirt which was his only garment, drawn over them inclosing his entire figure… This image and my fear entered into a species of combination with each other. That shape am I, I felt, potentially. Nothing that I possess can defend me against that fate, if the hour for it should strike for me as it struck for him. There was such a horror of him, and such a perception of my own momentary discrepancy from him, that it was as if something hitherto solid within my breast gave way entirely, and I became a mass of quivering fear. After this the universe was changed for me altogether. I awoke morning after morning with a horrible dread at the pit of my stomach, and with a sense of insecurity of life that I never knew before, and that I have never felt since.[1]

James learned a great deal about himself and humanity and found himself clinging to two convictions: "the thought of my having a will and of my belonging to the brotherhood of men."[2] These are extraordinary convictions for pulling us out of our dread and bringing us home. The reality and priority of the will and the liberty gained in discovering it and exercising it changed his life and gave it new direction. A new path opened up before him when he began to appreciate the common humanity he shared with others. In short, James discovered that human beings belong to each other and have real choices. Moreover, what they choose makes a difference to themselves and to others.

This "dreadful" experience with the epileptic boy has a sense of holiness about it. James came face to face with the fragility of things and with his own panic and the hope of rescue. It is to this sense of holy dread that the story of Jesus speaks. The Passion of Christ is the story of how God longs to heal and to forgive. James could, one supposes, have coped with his dread by developing a callous disposition. That is the route many in his position might have taken. He could have looked at the boy and, instead of making a radical identification with him, distanced himself from him. Something in James sensed that such distancing would have meant the death of his soul. We find Dante's hell populated with souls who dealt with their dread in this way. Dante's souls suffered from a kind of sclerosis of the heart. Sclerosis of the heart is what happens to us when we wall ourselves up. The self left to itself becomes a howling wilderness.

Harry Williams, emerging from a place of dread and terror in himself, wrote:

Most people's wilderness is inside them, not outside. Thinking of it outside is usually a trick we play on ourselves— a trick to hide from us what we really are, not comfortingly wicked, but incapable, for the time being, of establishing communion. Our wilderness, then, is an inner isolation. It's an absence of contact. It's a sense of being alone—boringly alone, or saddeningly alone, or terrifyingly alone.[3]

W. H. Auden, in his Advent poem *For the Time Being*, writes of the howling wilderness in the human heart that is not transformed by holiness.

*If we were never alone or always too busy,
Perhaps we might even believe what we know is not true:
But no one is taken in, at least not all of the time;
In our bath, or the subway, or the middle of the night,
We know very well we are not unlucky but evil... [4]*

To know that "we are not unlucky but evil" is hard to take. A scapegoat must be found. Religious people who cannot face their own capacity for evil turn God into a monster. Such a "God" becomes part of their and our punishment. In the words of the poet Edwin Muir, God becomes three angry letters in a book:

The Word made flesh here is made word again,
a word made word in flourish and arrogand crook,
see here King Calvin with his iron pen,
And God three angry letters in a book,
And there the logical hook
On which the Mystery is impaled and bent
Into an ideological instrument.

When God's mystery is impaled, so is ours. Religion degenerates into a cruel instrument of dread with which we clobber ourselves and other people. The message of Jesus is simple and can reach us in whatever "hell" our fear and dread may have placed us. God has fallen in love with you and wants you to come home!

There is a legend concerning Judas Iscariot. Judas, having betrayed Christ for thirty pieces of silver, went out and hanged himself. After this, Judas found himself at the bottom of a dark and dank pit. He lay there on his stomach for a million years. (Since he was in eternity, he experienced "time" in his own peculiar way.) Slowly and painfully he turned himself over on his back and lay in the darkness for another million years. He then saw, or thought he saw, a faint light miles above him at the mouth of the pit. Something in him drew him towards the light, or was it the light itself that did the drawing? He couldn't tell. With great difficulty, he stood up and began to climb. For years and years he climbed. Often he slipped back and had to wait a century or two to regain his strength to go on. As he climbed, the light grew stronger, and the closer he got to the mouth of the pit, the more Judas drew strength from the light. Eventually, after many aeons, he pulled himself over the edge and, much to his astonishment, he found himself in an Upper Room where a young rabbi was having a meal with his friends. The young rabbi came over to him, helped him to his feet and said, "Judas! Welcome! We've been waiting for you. We couldn't continue the supper without you."

God, in Jesus, is the one who waits and waits with infinite patience. He is still waiting. Please come home! Allow your dread to become holy. It will bring you back to the place of healing and peace. When we look at Jesus, something begins to move in us, just as the light drew Judas to his reunion with his friends. What draws us to Jesus is his radical identification with us. He is as weak and vulnerable as we are. In Jesus, we are able to pay attention to our frailty and restlessness. We find ourselves in "soul country." When we connect with our greatest weakness, we are suddenly very close to the heart of things. The restless heart, caught up in holy dread, knows that not even the one it loves most in the human realm, nor even the universe itself, can answer its deepest needs. God is the only One who satisfies and who, in satisfying us, draws us into an even deeper longing. Holy dread is God's way of trying to reach us. God uses us in all our fragility and doubt to be his word, to speak to us about ourselves.

James Hillman suggests that for there to be any opening in the soul for healing and growth there has to be an admission of weakness and the breakdown of the Western ego.

> *It's only when that breaks down, when… you can't get up and do it. When impotence happens and you can't get on with it. When you feel beaten, oppressed, knocked back… then something moves and you begin to feel yourself as a soul. You don't feel yourself as a soul when you're making it and doing it.*[5]

This was precisely the experience of William James. In the spring of 1870 his dreadful experience of not "making it and doing it" caused him to discover his soul. Hillman goes so far as to say that today "we are living in a psychic concentration camp, in the sense that we are passively accepting the soulless world."[6]

Perhaps this is the peculiar characteristic of the twentieth century? Is our era marked by the repression of soul? Studdert Kennedy, a distinguished chaplain in the First World War, wrote the European man,

> *the fiercest of the beasts of prey, who is not likely to abandon the weapons which have made him the lord and bully of the planet, is threatened with extinction unless he becomes a*

more tyrannous lord, using without restraint or remorse the
powers of destruction that have been put into his hands, or
dies with Christ, and finds a more excellent way.

We can now include American along with European man.
When our dread is not transformed into a holy dread it leads to
tyranny. We see that tyranny not only in the accumulation of
weapons of devastation by the so-called great powers (better to call
them great weaknesses) but also in "the terrifying corporation
mind, economics replacing value… Cost-efficiency means the most
return for the least investment: well, that's psychopathic, a moral
deficiency and getting away with it."[7]

There is, therefore, much that we have to give up if we are to
find our way home. Coming home means the dismantling of the
old self, and this is truly dreadful. William James found his old self
in ruins in the face of his identification with the epileptic boy.
Which way shall we go? The way of callousness, which is death, or
the way of transformation, which feels like death at first but which
is the path to life in all its fullness?

Lent is traditionally a period of testing, a time of temptation.
Temptations serve a very important role in our coming home to
ourselves, to one another, and to God. Temptation is a kind of
questioning of present arrangements, present realities. We say to
ourselves, "I don't like the way things are. What would happen if I
were to do thus and such?" By suggesting something to us, temptation has a way of disconcerting us and makes us be in touch with
our longings and our shame in a very unsettling way. Father André
Louf writes that because

it opens a breach and dismantles something within us,
temptation brings with it the possibility of a rich outpouring
grace, and growth in the Holy Spirit. If we can bring our-
selves to accept this dismantling and to appear in all our
weakness and poverty, these will very soon be replaced and
taken over by the power of God which works to the full in our
weakness.[8]

I have to confess that this is not the kind of God I particularly like. There is absolutely no room for a freewheeling, autonomous me, in charge of my own destiny and captain of my soul. Still, I would very soon get tired of a God of my own invention. This is the only way I come up against that which I cannot control, manipulate, and absorb into my own little world. I need this stretching, because I sense places inside me that do not yet exist, and it is necessary for suffering to penetrate these in order that they can come to term and be born.

Without holy dread and the encounter with myself as frail and weak, my life becomes a game of Trivial Pursuit. My trivial way of believing and my trivial sense of self go together. The paradox is that, the more I learn to surrender my self, a more generous and available me comes into existence. When I concentrate on my self, the less there is of me.

Sim Goodchild in William Golding's *Darkness Visible* was a man who had lost his way and knew it. He knew he was far from "home" and from time to time he

sat at the back [of his shop] and tried to think of First Things... he knew that after a moment or two on First Things (getting back, he sometimes called it) he knew he would be likely to find himself brooding on the fact that he was too fat, also as bald as bald... bald, old and breathless.[9]

The human heart, when left to itself, inclines to dissatisfaction and is easily distracted from its true home. We concentrate on the loss of our powers, our looks, our ability to control events. We become mesmerized by the triviality of it all. Sim Goodchild's attempt to "get back" was depressing failure. All he got back to was his lost and fragmented self.

[He] at this point began silently to rehearse his own partic-ular statement [of belief]. It is all reasonable. It is equally unreasonable. I believe it all as much as I believe anything that is out of sight; as I believe in the expanding universe,

which is to say as I believe in the Battle of Hastings, as I believe in the life of Jesus, as I believe in... It is a kind of belief which touches nothing in me. It is a kind of second-class believing. My beliefs are me; many and trivial.[10]

Our trouble is that we do not want to be in constant touch with our profound weakness and vulnerability. Still less do we believe that a new energy for living comes when we begin to live *from* them. We *do* find an energy within of a particularly calculating and destructive kind when we try to live with a lonely and fragmented self. In fact, such energy is the engine of much activity in our society. It fuels the cycle of "getting and spending." It sends the addictive and acquisitive on the road that leads away from home. The path to perdition is scattered with the detritus of our trivial pursuits.

The way back home (through the recovery of holy dread) is through the door of imaginative compassion. If Sim Goodchild had been able to move out of himself into the world of others experiencing the same kind of loneliness, he would have made a radical turn in the direction of home. The poet Stevie Smith puts a refrain in the mouth of a drowned man on the beach. The bathers are gathered round the corpse. They hadn't noticed him. The dead man's cry is, "I wasn't waving but drowning!" We aren't very good at interpreting one another's signals. Many are drowning because we are far from home, and when we are far from home we are far from God and each other.

There is a Hasidic story concerning the Baal Shem Tov, the great founder of Hasidism, that uses the metaphor of drowning to explain the gestures and body movements of those in prayer.

When a man is drowning in the river, and splashes about trying to pull himself out of the waters that are overwhelming him, those who see him will certainly not make fun of his splashing. So, when a man prays with gestures, there is no reason to make fun of him, for he is saving himself from the raging waters that come upon him to distract him from his prayer.

I wasn't waving but drowning! We not only mistake one another's signals, we are also in danger of making fun of one another's splashing.

In the Story of the Passion we find ourselves in a different world. God's signals are clear. What could be clearer than the cross? What could be clearer as a sign for how we are to love one another? Who would not be filled with either revulsion or holy dread? God's vulnerability teaches us that the way home is by learning to be at the service of others. We are to wait and watch with each other, not out of some self-deceptive "messiah complex" but out of the knowledge that we awaken in each other things of the soul that would never come to be. Without you, I cannot happen. Without you, I cannot find my way home. God on the cross places us in each other's care.

There is a story that a holy man, a Sufi, was so advanced in the spiritual life that he knew God's secret purpose for us. In this tale, Allah addressed the Sufi, Abu'l-Hassan al-Kharraqani, saying, "Shall I tell the people of thy spiritual drunkennes so that, being scandalized, they will stone thee?" The Sufi's "drunkenness" was his advancement in prayer and his lack of reliance on outward forms. So confident was he in his discovery of Allah's secret purpose that he answered instantly, "Shall I tell the people of thine infinite Mercy that they will never again bow down to thee in prayer?" God's "secret" is that God loves us unconditionally and has made the world in such a way that we all belong to one another. God's mercy is such that in God all things "move and have their being."

Alice Walker's heroine in *The Color Purple* knew something of the infinite mercy of God when she discovered the solidarity of all things:

It ain't something you can look at apart from anything else, including yourself… My first step from the old white man [God] was trees. Then air. Then birds. Then other people. But one day when I was sitting quiet and feeling like a motherless child, which I was, it come to me: that feeling of being part of everything, not separate at all. I knew that if I cut a tree, my arm would bleed.[11]

The insight that if she cut a tree her arm would bleed is a turning toward home. The road leads to a bleeding tree. The cross is the place where all things meet, where you can't understand yourself apart from everyone and everything else. God's Passion is ours, too. The three little words, *love one another*, are full of holy dread, because they speak of God's longing for us. St. Ignatius of Antioch cried these "dreadful" words of passion about God's Passion.

Him I seek who died for me.
Him I desire who rose for me.
The birth pangs are upon me!

Homecoming! The metaphors about it are many and varied but none more full of holy dread than the image of giving birth. God's mercy is such that he invites us to be co-creators with him of each other. Lent is the time when we are forged into a people who, because we are going home, can afford to give ourselves away to each other and to the world.

STUDY QUESTIONS

1. Jones writes of William James's touching the rock bottom of depression and discovering "that human beings belong to each other and have real choices. Moreover, what they choose makes a difference to themselves and to others" (p. 90). What effects did this discovery have on James? How might you respond when discovering this responsibility and connection?

2. Reread the legend Jones cites on page 92 concerning Judas Iscariot. Read it aloud. What effect does this legend have on you?

3. According to Jones, "God is the only One who satisfies and who, in satisfying us, draws us into an even deeper longing" (p. 93). He also quotes Father André Louf that because "it opens a breach and dismantles something within us, temptation brings with it the possibility of a rich outpouring of grace, and growth in the Holy Spirit" (p. 94). Explore the tensions established by these ideas. What might be a logical response? What emotions do they elicit in you?

4. "Our trouble," Jones writes, "is that we do not want to be in constant touch with our profound weakness and vulnerability" (p. 96). What costs come with the constant awareness of our weakness and vulnerability? What are the promises?

5. Jones uses homecoming to describe the experience of an ever-deepening sense of relationship with God. What homecomings have you lived in your life? How do they shape your understanding of Jones's images?

8.

HOME MEANS FREEDOM
TO BECOME A FAMILY

We are in the week of Crucifixion, and it is hard to understand what road to Golgotha leads home to our greatest joy. It is the road to freedom. The image of home plays a large role in the games we play and the sporting activities we enjoy. People display extraordinary loyalty to the "home team" and love the "moral clarity" of team sports. In fact, metaphors taken from baseball, football, and other sports are not only found in everyday speech about "the game of life" but also provide a way of talking about religious commitment.

When I was growing up in England, sporting images took on moral and religious significance. That could account for my never being very good at sports! The moral weight was too much. Cricket was the summer game of my youth. George Orwell wrote, "It is not a twentieth-century game, and nearly all modern-minded people dislike it. The Nazis for instance…"[1] I was never any good at cricket, but I admired the game. It still reminds me of lazy, civilized summer afternoons of my boyhood. I am glad that the Nazis never took to it! I remember coming across an old book called *The Cricket Field of the Christian Life* (published in 1910). The author, the Reverend Thomas Waugh, described the Christian life as a kind of cricket match. The two teams were the Christians and the unbelievers; the two captains, Jesus Christ and the Devil. God was the umpire (referee). The good thing about the game was that the result was a foregone conclusion! It was important to be on the winning team, and the book was an invitation to the young player (attracted by the seductive offerings of the Devil) to change sides.

Put your whole soul into the game, and make it your very life. Hit clean and hard at every loose ball… be alert and you will run up a grand score. And, when "time" is called you will "bring out your bat," your own conscience will say, "Well done!" and those you have cheered and helped will say, "A good man! Thank God for such an inning!" Aye, and when on the resurrection morning you come out of the pavilion, leaving your playing clothes behind you, and robed like your glorious Captain-King, you and all the hosts of God will see and understand your score as you cannot now, and your joy will be full as you hear the Captain, the innumerable company of angels and the whole Church of God greet you with the words, "WELL PLAYED, SIR!"

I have to admit that, while I still find the metaphor funny, the strong belief behind it speaks to a very deep part of me and shows up my easygoing cynicism for what it is. There is a moral clarity and courage here that I find challenging. Have I made my pilgrimage "my very life"? Have I lived my life as passionately and as clearly as the would-be cricketer?

Similar questions floated in my mind not long ago when my ten-year-old son and I went to a key varsity basketball game. We loved it, and it wouldn't take much for me to get addicted. It was lucky that on this occasion we were rooting for the winning team. For two hours we lived life without any ambiguity! No wonder team games are important for millions. There was no doubt in our minds about *who* should win. Life had no grey areas. Everything was crystal clear—at least for those magical two hours. We even knew which side God was on, and when our team won, God was vindicated! We felt at home in the world, and all was well. During the game, we experienced two emotions that do not always go together in everyday life. We felt free, *and* we felt that we belonged. We had been given a glimpse of heaven!

My son and I eventually had to come down to earth. We had to drive across the Bay Bridge into San Francisco and return to a world in which God is not so easily vindicated. It is not always easy to see God at work in the world. God is neither so obvious nor so manageable as popular religion proclaims. As we have seen, pilgrims to Easter have to face some hard facts about themselves before God is revealed. We live in a world in which people are *not* divided up into the righteous and the unrighteous as in a basketball game. At first glance, given the evils in the world, there is no way that God can be justified. Someone (looking at the suffering in the world) once said, "The only possible excuse God could have would be not to exist!" Our anger and disappointment seem justified. Things are not as they should be, and if God isn't responsible then who is?

One of the hardest things for people to admit is their secret hatred of God. Hatred of and disappointment in God underlie a great deal of what passes for unbelief. They are also common among many people who consider themselves religious. "God" is continually letting then down by not doing what he is supposed to do. People believe, but resent what they believe. Hatred of God, however, can be a very important stage in our homecoming. William Butler Yeats wrote, "I study hatred—a passion in my own control." Hatred is a dangerous route back to God, but one that many have to take.

Then my delivered soul herself shall learn
A darker knowledge and in hatred turn
From every thought of God mankind has had.
Thought is a garment and the soul a bride
That cannot in that trash and tinsel hide.
Hatred of God may bring the soul to God.[2]

The pilgrimage we call Lent places us in a crucible of love that purges away the trash and tinsel of our thoughts and feelings about God. We may even have to get to the stage of "hating God," or, better, "hating" the idol we worship instead of God. What we worship is often a trashy (vindictive or sentimental, according to our mood and training) "God" made to our own specifications. We live in a culture that specializes in custom-built gods for personal use. Westerners have often been guilty of judging other forms of belief in parts of the world in a supercilious way. Christians have denigrated non-Christians for worshiping many gods and for indulging in what looks like superstitious practices.

But our pantheon is no less crowded and our behavior no more rational that that of other peoples. Lent is a time when I have to unlearn everything and try to see the world with unprejudiced eyes. My beliefs are corrupted by my need to look down on others. The various "dead ends" on the pilgrimage serve a great purpose. They are opportunities to see the trash and tinsel of religion and of the culture for what they are. "Hatred of God" may bring the soul to God through a passionate process of stripping away all that prevents us from seeing clearly. The "unlearning" process begins by asking old questions with new vigor. Where is God to be found? How can God be vindicated? Is it possible to be free? The main issue for pilgrims is that of freedom. We want to be home free. We long for it. As we have seen, in order to be free we have to face our capacity for evil and acknowledge our longing for love. Both our capacity and our longing get us into trouble. But unless we are willing to face this kind of trouble we shall never discover who we are and what we are about. We long for a world where there is only certainty and no ambiguity. We want to be citizens of a clear and well-ordered kingdom, but the moral clarity of the basketball game only lasts two hours.

It is not accidental that the pilgrimage brings us to the point of resentment and even hatred where we are sorely tested and tempted. The place of tempting and temptation is, after all, where the followers of Jesus would expect to find themselves more often than not. The first action of the Holy Spirit in Jesus' adult life was to drive him into the wilderness. It is not only the preparation for an active and wonderful ministry, it is also the foretaste of the last journey to Jerusalem.

Jesus is led by the Spirit to be tempted by Satan. He is involved in a struggle about freedom, evil, and love. What the story of the temptations is trying to teach us is that the theater of our becoming human is the wilderness that we dread. The three temptations correspond to human needs. When they are not immediately satisfied we grow resentful. Turning stones into bread for the hungry seems to be a miracle that would do no harm in a world where children are crying out for bread. God, however, does not respond to our longing for miracles of this sort. Something in me wonders why Jesus, when the devil showed him the kingdoms of the world and told him to take charge, did not lead a political revolution. The cry for a leader points to one of our deepest desires. We may not want to be in charge ourselves, but we dearly wish that someone was. A world in chaos needs a strong ruler. This deep desire of ours for an orderly world is rejected by God in favor of another Way, which leads us to a dark place of dereliction. God won't even allow Jesus to be an unequivocal sign to the nations. The Devil goes on to suggest that Jesus throw himself off the pinnacle of the Temple. A wonder-worker would compel belief. We like to be on the winning side, and we want it to be obvious that we are with the winners. We don't like losers. Being a loser might be catching. That is why we distance ourselves from failure. Jesus chooses to be a failure, chooses to follow a path away from easy solutions and the working of the kind of miracles that would compel belief. We follow him on another Way. Here we are in the week of Crucifixion. It is a time of transformation. Imagine yourself as a giant chrysalis, hard and brittle on the outside, waiting for the inner life to burst forth.

The road through the wilderness has led us to the foot of the cross. We have gone through the untried and the unknown only to find ourselves at "the place of a skull," a crucible of transformation. We would rather not go on. We would rather be unslaved by an unthinking certainty, and there is plenty of the trashy and tinselly kind of religion to give us what we want.

Think about your basic needs. As we have seen, we long for the kind of moral clarity that we can enjoy for the two hours spent at the ball game. We long to have someone keep our conscience so that we are relieved of the responsibility of having to think things through. The temptation is to imagine that we can ever get to a place where we don't have to struggle anymore with the ambiguities and uncertainties of life. Our longing for miracle, authority, and mystery was prefigured in the temptations of Jesus in the wilderness. He turned his back on them and made his way to Jerusalem. We must do the same. Our longing for miracle, authority, and mystery can easily be exploited by those who peddle magic, tyranny, and mystification. Think of your own temptation to be enslaved by what you perceive to be your needs. Think how open you are to the tyranny of some form of mystification.

Think about your *God-given* vulnerability. It is a gift! It makes you available to God and to others. All our adventures on the Pilgrims' Way have been to help us see the gift in our vulnerability. We live in the faith of God's love and not in the "certainty" of our own position. We can now catch a glimpse of the fact there may well be a kind of certainty from which we would like to be saved. There is the kind of certainty that kills the passion in the heart. It would have us all marching the goose step down the great road of life, in serried ranks, all cloned from a "true believer," all with the same fixed smile. But that isn't what we are about. The freedom won on the cross brings with it both doubt and responsibility. That is why we dread it.

Our culture is notorious for its *claim* to be free, yet it refuses to accept the burden of freedom. We go on extending the boundaries of irresponsibility. For example, there is a tendency to extend the definition of what constitutes a mental illness. This is one of the many ways in which we expand the area of irresponsibility. We fail to see the corresponding diminishment of our freedom. With every claim we make when we say, "I couldn't help it. It's not my fault, I'm not responsible" (when we could, when it was, and when we are), we mortgage our freedom in the name of security and safety. We do it all in the name of making ourselves "at home." When I shun responsibility, I condemn myself to solitary confinement. I lose my freedom and cut myself off from others. I am left "at home" with myself, and that is hell. Home, if it is to mean anything, has to be with others. Home means family. Home means solidarity with Creation. Home means freedom.

In Fyodor Dostoyevski's *The Brothers Karamazov,* Ivan tells his brother Alyosha the story of the Grand Inquisitor to make the point that freedom is the last thing human beings want. As a prelude to his story, Ivan tells his brother of his rebellion against God. He recounts a terrible incident when a general, living in splendor on his estate, commits an act of unspeakable bestiality.

He has kennels of hundreds of hounds and nearly a hundred dog-boys—all mounted and in uniform. One day a serf boy, a little boy of eight, threw a stone in play and hurt the paw of the general's favorite hound… He was taken—taken from his mother and locked up all night… The child is brought from the lock-up. It's a gloomy cold, foggy autumn day, a capital day for hunting. The general orders the child to be undressed; the child is stripped naked… "Make him run," commands the general. "Run! Run!" shout the boys. The boy runs… "At him!" yells the general, and he sets the whole pack of hounds on the child. The hounds catch him, and tear him to pieces before his mother's eyes.[3]

Ivan hastens to return his ticket "home" to the God who would allow such things. The God of Christianity has a great deal to answer for. It is God who needs to be forgiven! Who would want to come home to a God who permits the evils of the world, who allows the innocent to suffer? This kind of God has to be either malevolent or powerless.

We may not know, first hand, of acts of bestiality that match that of the general setting his dogs on the little boy, but we know of other tragedies that touch us and our friends. A few years ago a friend of ours, a talented and brilliant member of the New York City Ballet, threw himself out of his apartment window. We were stunned. He had everything to live for. Why would this splendid artist take his own life? When we are forced to work through the anger and grief that such tragedies bring, we are stripped naked. Joe's death was pointless. He was a man in whom "the Lord delighted." His art was his life. It was a prayer. And now he has gone, and I still don't know why. The anger wells up in me, years later, even as I write about it. I know something of the outrage of an Ivan Karamazov.

C. S. Lewis was stripped bare when his wife, Joy, died. A neatly packaged, problem-solving Christianity was no help. Treating faith as a narcotic did not work. The pain wouldn't go away. His little home was blown away. Lewis wrote:

If my house has collapsed at one blow, that is because it was a house of cards. If I had really cared, as I thought I did, about the sorrows of the world, I should have not been over-whelmed when my own sorrow came. It has been an imaginary faith, innocuous counters marked "illness," "pain," "death," "loneliness." I thought I trusted the rope until it mattered to me whether it would bear me or not. Now it matters and I find that it didn't.

The winds of Holy Week howl around the ruins of our fragile dwellings and show up our imaginary faith for what it is. We are at a place where there are no easy answers. Is there anything or anyone that holds us in being? Perhaps there is really nothing there at all? The howling wind groans in the depths of our own souls and demands that we cease treating life as a game that will go on forever and take ourselves seriously. This doesn't mean taking ourselves too seriously (which is simply yet another narcissistic ploy of the ego) but realizing that the stakes are high. Life is not a cricket match or a game of basketball. What we do *matters*. Emily Dickinson wrote:

But should the play prove piercing earnest,
Should the glee glaze in death's despair,
Would not the fun look too expensive?
Would not the jest have crawled too far?

Much of our fun and jesting masks an underlying sense of hopelessness. But we are not alone. We are with other pilgrims throughout the ages who know that our sense of dread is a condition of freedom, part of the life of faith. The joy and sheer unexpectedness of being alive, the "dreadful" understanding of ourselves as experimental and provisional, the sense that we are always at risk—these are the conditions of freedom.

The conditions of freedom are simple. Covenant is the first. To be Pilgrims of the Covenant means our caring for each other in God in the face of wonder and death. Abraham and Sarah, as we have seen, are our "parents in faith." They were willing to become God's great experiment, an experiment that is still going on. Abraham and Sarah's family is still in the making and includes all people. The second condition of our freedom follows from the first. We are citizens of a country, the boundaries of which are always expanding. "Home" is where everyone is welcome. There is room for everybody. Yet Jesus weeps over our little common-wealths because of their injustices. "O, Jerusalem, Jerusalem, killing the prophets and stoning those who are sent to you! How often would I have gathered your children together as a hen gathers her brood under her wings, and you would not! Behold, your house is forsaken. And I tell you, you will not see me until you say, 'Blessed be he who comes in the name of the Lord'" (see Luke 13:31–35, RSV). If the acceptance of a covenant relationship with God and the entry into an ever-expanding fellowship are the first two requirements of freedom, then weeping over our sins as Jesus wept over Jerusalem is the third. Our longing for freedom and a true homecoming leads us right into the pain and Passion of God.

If we are to be truly free, we have to be willing to be citizens of a Commonwealth that God is building in God's Passion and pain. The drama of the Passion stretches our understanding to its limits. Old meanings are dislocated, wrenched from their moorings. During the week of Crucifixion we have to think the unthinkable. God weeps! God suffers! God is Victim! A rabbi writing in the first century has God ask extraordinary question of the angels, "I love human beings so much that I want to identify with them in their pain. Tell me, how do I mourn?" God seeks instruction on how to weep! God, in Christ, identifies with us. If we would be truly free and at home, we are to share in the life of a God who weeps, who suffers, who identifies with the poorest and most wretched among us. The question for Holy Week, the Week of Passion, is, Do you really want to share in the life of such a God?

The answer of an Ivan Karamazov is a resounding No! Ivan's outrage is the engine that drives the story of the Grand Inquisitor. It is set in Seville at the height of the Spanish Inquisition. Jesus has returned to earth and raises a seven-year-old child from the dead.

The Grand Inquisitor, almost ninety years old, summons the guards and has Jesus arrested. Later that night the old man comes to visit his prisoner. Jesus never says a word. The old man asks,

"Why... art Thou come to hinder us?... [T]omorrow I shall condemn Thee and burn Thee at the stake as the worst of heretics. And the very people who have kissed Thy feet, tomorrow at the faintest sign from me will rush to heap up the embers of Thy fire... Thou wouldst go into the world, and art going with empty hands, with some promise of freedom which men in their simplicity and their natural unruliness cannot even understand, which they fear and dread—for nothing has ever been more insupportable for a man and a human society than freedom... Tomorrow I shall burn Thee."

When the Inquisitor ceased speaking he waited some time for his Prisoner to answer him. His silence weighed down upon him. He saw that the Prisoner had listened intently all the time... The old man longed for Him to say something, however bitter and terrible. But He suddenly approached the old man in silence and softly kissed him on his bloodless aged lips. That was all his answer. The old man shuddered. His lips moved. He went to the door, opened it, and said to Him: "Go, and come no more... Come not at all, never, never!"[4]

The Inquisitor believed that the way of freedom is too hard for human beings. It is too much to ask them to be experiments in vulnerability. It is as if he was saying, "We priests have to correct your work. A free man or woman can never be happy. Don't you understand that? Human beings don't want freedom. They want to be looked after and told what to believe. They don't want your terrible gift of freedom. Those weren't temptations in the wilderness. They were the voice of common sense. You turned your back on humanity and chose a harder way, an impossible way. And now it has led you to your own destruction. You are on the road to Calvary. And you deserve to die, because you not only brought us the promise of freedom but you also gave us its burdensome twin, doubt. Human beings don't want to wander in the wilderness of freedom and doubt. They want to be safe at home." The Grand Inquisitor saw his fellow human beings as in deep need for order. Each needed "someone to worship, someone to keep his conscience, and some means of uniting all in one unanimous and harmonious ant-heap."

The Inquisitor did not understand that we are not ants and that our way home to God and to each other must pass through the wilderness of freedom and doubt. Otherwise there is no real homecoming at all. We live with the illusion that our safe cell is our destination. Cut off from God and from each other, we try to make ourselves at home. Money helps. Alcohol helps. Security helps. All our addictions help us forget where we really are. But there is something deep within us that is trying to stay awake, something in us that aches for a true homecoming. Even in the heart of the Grand Inquisitor something is capable of being touched.

The end of the story is significant. Alyosha asks Ivan, "And the old man?" "The kiss glows in his heart, but the old man adheres to his idea." The silence and the kiss of Jesus are often all we get as signs that we are on pilgrimage home. Even as the kiss glows in our heart we, like the Inquisitor, can say No! to it.

Elie Wiesel, the eloquent Jewish writer and commentator, bears witness to the drama that is played out in the human heart. He was once asked about the difficulty of believing in God after the experience of the Holocaust. Is belief possible after Auschwitz? Wiesel responded that if it was hard to live in a world without faith in God, it was even harder to live a life of faith. If you want difficulties, choose to live with God. "The real drama is the drama of the believer!"

Holy Week is the beginning of the Drama of the Believer. It is the drama of freedom. One of the reasons we resist freedom is that it makes life provisional, experimental, and open—open to risk. The Inquisitor is right. The experimental nature of freedom means that it is not a private matter. The dominant image of the Old Testament is that of *covenant*, the bond between God and his People. Whatever our freedom is, it is manifested in and only through relationship with God and with each other. This kind of freedom builds up community. It is political. St. Paul (in Phil. 3:20) insists that "our commonwealth is in heaven." The idea of heavenly or otherworldly "politics" is very dangerous. Some people like the idea of a Christianity that is not concerned with the affairs of this world but is focused on a sort of private arrangement with God for their own safety and happiness. The phrase *our commonwealth is in heaven* means that true freedom involves a covenant that binds us to the God who weeps, who suffers and who dies.

There is no way around the Passion. Meister Eckehart wrote, "If you want to be a child of God and you do not want to suffer, you are all wrong. When our Lord said, 'Let him deny himself and take up his cross and follow me' (Matt. 16:24), that means let him become that same one that I am." To be a child of God is to know the meaning of suffering and delight. To be a child of God is to enter the mystery of the Passion and become a divine experiment in vulnerability. Our pain is the pain of new life seeking to burst out in us—a life that embraces everyone.

We have come a long way from the divine cricket match or the moral clarity of the basketball game. We have come a long way toward finding our true home. We get that much closer when we face the dread that the promise of freedom and faith brings. We get closer as we accept ourselves as experiments in vulnerability. We get even closer when we are able to receive the healing words, *Come home. All is forgiven!*

Study Questions

1. Jones opens this chapter with references to "moral clarity." What about this concept is attractive to you? What might a cynical viewpoint be?

2. Jones tells of enjoying a varsity basketball game with his son. He writes, "…we experienced two emotions that do not always go together in everyday life. We felt free, *and* we felt that we belonged. We had been given a glimpse of heaven!" (p. 101). How does this image of heaven compare with others you have known? When have you experienced both a feeling of freedom and a sense of belonging? When have you worked to create such a hospitable atmosphere?

3. Jones writes of "'hating God,' or, better, 'hating' the idol we worship instead of God" (p. 102), and of how such a thing as this may bring the soul through "a passionate process of stripping away all that prevents us from seeing clearly" (p. 103). How would one go about engaging in this process? What safeguards would you want? Where might be a safe place for the expression of such hatred (in the church, to a close friend, in private writing, in prayer)?

4. "The God of Christianity has a great deal to answer for," asserts Jones (p. 106). This is "a God who weeps, who suffers, who identifies with the poorest and most wretched among us" (p. 108). "Do you really want to share in the life of such a God?" Why? Why not?

5. Jones writes of "the promise of freedom" and "its burdensome twin, doubt…." In what ways are the two related? Which plays a greater role in your life? Where is God in the balance between them?

9.
COME HOME!
ALL IS FORGIVEN!

I keep coming back to the image of my middle-aged friend who had found himself spontaneously saying over and over again, "I want to go home!" This longing for home opened up a new place in him, and he knew himself to be "an experiment in vulnerability." Holy Week, the greatest week of the Christian Year, during which the drama of God's vulnerability is played out, holds the secret of our homecoming. Our way home is through passion—our passion and God's.

At this time I feel like a cross between Ivan Karamazov and my friend. Part of me longs for home, while the other half is either doubtful of its existence or sees it as yet another occasion for disappointment and betrayal. In Holy Week, my annual quarrel with God comes to a head. It looks as if, yet again, God is going to make a fool of himself by betraying himself into our hands. What kind of God is manifested in the growing drama of this week? Like Ivan Karamazov I am inflicted by what I call my Judas complex. I feel as if I might, at any moment, be betrayed. I feel as if I might be made a fool of. Better anticipate the worst and betray rather than risk being betrayed. The betrayal of Christ by Judas had its roots in what was an understandable resentment. Jesus must have been a great disappointment to a great number of people. I look at the world, I look at my country, I look at myself. There rises up in me a voice that says, "Surely God could do better than this!" My disappointment easily slips into anger and resentment. Somewhere deep inside me (perhaps a wound of betrayal from childhood left its mark?) there comes a bitter cry, "Life isn't meant to be like this! It isn't meant to be full of pain and tragedy. I bet to return my ticket." If I am to enter into the mystery of God's Passion, I have to be committed to a ruthlessly honest exercise of memory. Remembering can be hard work. I spend a great deal of time and energy editorializing my life. I repress my memory. I conveniently forget things. I continually rewrite the script of my life. The rewriting is a dangerous undertaking, because the past, while capable of reinterpretation, cannot be undone. The past shapes our present experience and cannot be ignored. A friend of mine puts it this way: The self is what the past is doing now.

Holy Week is a time when I am given the opportunity to reflect on how my past infects and affects my present. There are memories that refuse to come to the surface. I catch a glimpse of them out of the corner of my eye. I know that they are there, but I don't always know what they are about, except that the pain issuing from them pushes me more and more into editing my life so that only the "good bits" show. I fool myself into thinking that I live only in the present and that the past has no effect on my life now.

I remember reading an arresting image of the marshmallows that we roast over the camp fire at vacation time. The writer (Lance Morrow of *Time* magazine) suggested that the marshmallow is a good image of the "self" in modern society. The marshmallow is thrust into the heat, the roasted outside eaten, and what is left plunged into the fire again. This procedure is followed until the marshmallow disappears in one last delicious roasted bite. So it is with our lives. We burn up and begin again, burn up and begin again until there is nothing left. Americans can always start over. We behave as if the past doesn't count. Morrow called this attitude "the doctrine of discontinuous selves." But to be a "self" (or, better, to have a soul) means to have a sense of continuity. This is why memory is important.

The memory that Holy Week seeks to revive is one that lies deep within everyone. It is the memory of our beginnings. It is *the* memory that enables us to remember the painful things of our past without despair. The Great Memory is simply this: *God has fallen in love with you and wants you to come home!* Our first memory is God's love for us, and it is that memory that has been buried and repressed. Your first memory (if only you could get back to it) is that of being God's joy and delight. Why is it difficult to remember the joy of our beginnings in the heart of God? I wonder if it has something to do with our unwillingness to face the fact of our limited future? Memory and hope are intimately related. Perhaps we cannot recall the love that brought us into being in the first place, because we cannot imagine a love strong enough to pull us through the gate of death. I refuse to remember, because I dare not hope. I refuse to remember and I dare not hope, because I am frightened and angry because I will have to change. W. H. Auden's words speak to me.

We would rather be ruined than changed.
We would rather die in our dread
Than climb the cross of the moment
And see our illusions die.

Each year I feel as if I am invited to have an encounter not only with my faulty memory but also with the unknown, to dive ever more deeply into my own ignorance. Abraham Heschel suggests there are two kinds of ignorance. "One is insipid, caused by negligence, oversight; the other lucid, the result of diligence, insight. The one leads to vanity and complacency; the other to humility and understanding."[1] The exposure of my ignorance is God's way of putting me on the road to wisdom. My ignorance takes on something of the second variety. It is transformed into the instrument by which I realize that I am a mystery to myself. It is as if I am caught up in a whirlwind over which I have no control. I am in a new world apprehended in faith and governed by grace. I am in the world of the Passion of God. I am in the world of fire and wind. Rebellion like that of Ivan Karamazov is as futile as sentimental affirmations of meaning. I find myself in the place beyond argument. The whirlwind of God does not compel belief. It simply *is*. I can always say No! The simple fact is that the idea of negotiating with a whirlwind is absurd. God's whirlwind carries us home. Its refreshing energy heals our wounds.

"Now when the Lord was about to take Elijah up to heaven by a whirlwind…" (2 Kings 2:1–15, RSV). What a fantastic way to begin a story! Elijah is one of my favorite characters in the Old

Testament. There is also passion and excitement in the story that stirs something inside me to ask the question, How am I going to die—clinically and alone or with the chariots and horses of fire? Of course, I am only talking in images. (How else are we to speak of the things that touch us deeply?) The images are signs of something profound and abidingly real. The question, How am I going to die? raises for me another even more urgent one: How am I going to live? If the Christian religion is about anything it is about the true source of life and our need to sniff out where it is. A sense of smell is essential, because patterns of death are easily made up to look like promises of life. Death is, at times, a brilliant cosmetician.

The story of the Ascension of Elijah is about the passing on of life. It has its funny side in that Elijah spends a great deal of his time trying to lose Elisha, or rather to test him to see if he is in earnest about being a prophet. Elisha asks for a double share of Elijah's spirit. In order to receive it, he has to take care not to miss the main event. "And as they still went on and talked, behold, a chariot of fire and horses of fire separated the two of them. And Elijah went up by a whirlwind into heaven." To understand where the sources of life and vitality are we have to be like Elisha: expect great things from God as Mystery and be continually attentive.

We live in an age that is appallingly ignorant with regard to Christianity understood as a *mystery*. By mystery I do not mean something vague and woolly but rather an acknowledgment of the stupendous reality in which we live and move and have our being. The ignorance (of the insipid and negligent variety) of this mystery is nowhere more appalling than among some of Christianity's most vigorous practitioners. Christianity has largely lost its ability to surprise. There is no fire. This is because our profound ignorance is covered with a thick layer of supposed familiarity. Holy Week restores the element of surprise by not only showing us God's Passion but by throwing us (if we so choose) into the midst of action.

One teacher rightly complains of the fact that it is hard for students "to sense on their pulse the reality of Christianity as a tradition which was alive in the past and lives today."[2] I would also direct his complaint against Christianity's most vociferous exponents in our culture. TV evangelists shout and scream as if there were no Christian history, no differing and even contradictory traditions, and only one way to walk. Christianity tends to be identified with three things that mislead us with regard to its abiding mystery. It is often identified with *institutions,* with *dogmas,* and with the *West.* These three are not to be discounted, but they do not begin to exhaust the mystery. Left to themselves, they tend to drain the drama of its vitality and passion. Even those who claim to have a personal, one-on-one relationship with Jesus Christ have been seduced by this three-fold identification. In many ways they are the most contaminated, because it is hard for them to see the difference between a personal commitment to Jesus Christ and to a whole set of largely unexamined values, dogmas, and institutions that bolster their way of life. This is in no way to deny that Jesus Christ changes lives. He does. The question is, How do you know the genuine article? How do you sniff out where life really is? How do you challenge the terrible discrepancy between faith and practice? Ivan Karamazov had a point. Christianity has a bad name in many places because of its tendency to give easy and shallow answers.

If we add to the scandal of a general moral decline in our culture the ambiguity of the Christian witness, the picture looks bleak. There was an advertisement recently in the magazine *Career Insights* (which is directed to college students, particularly seniors). It read: "In the 60s the word was love. In the 70s, it was peace. In the 80s, it's money. We can help you make it."

Such promises are made with regard to Christianity, too. To be a Christian is to make it, to be a success. Christianity becomes motivationally equivalent to Geritol. "Take this product regularly and you will be successful, youthfully middle-aged and always happy."[3] That, of course, is a cruel if attractive lie, and many religious people are trying to live that lie. Imagine the rage and disappointment seething beneath the surface. The attempt to live such lies explains, in part, the violence of our times. Christianity is still a popular and populist religion in the U.S.A. and that isn't all bad.

But there are countless people who would like to believe, who are, in fact, aching to believe, and who cannot because they imagine that they have to swallow a great deal of nonsense and even lies in order to do so. We long for the fire and passion of Elijah's ascension and the maturity in believing of which we read, for example, in the Letter to the Ephesians (4:1–7, 11–16), of our unity and giftedness in the Spirit that is luring us, calling us to "the measure of the stature of the fullness of Christ." Our living and our liveliness are found in our growing up into Christ—together, not alone. And Mystery, the unknown and unmanipulable, is the context and condition of our growing up. The pilgrimage of faith (with its promise of freedom) puts us in touch with our ignorance and vulnerability. It also makes us available to healing and newness.

When the Greek fathers of the early Church talked about us as being made after the image of God, they saw us as somehow unfinished and incomplete. This incompleteness is both our glory and our pain: our glory because there is always more to be revealed about each one of us—we advance "from glory to glory." There is pain because, like a wound, our incompleteness is a continual reminder that our destiny lies elsewhere. "Here we have no abiding city." We might put the two ideas of pain and glory together and say that a human being is one who is wounded by glory. You can catch a glimpse of it on the face of another at particular moments. The glory can be seen when a person, while remaining truly himself, rises above himself and is something more. It is this "something more" that we need to cherish and learn to love. Elisha takes on the mantle of Elijah and can be and do more than he imagined.

The writer to the Ephesians names this call to "something more," this pull of transcendence, a process of "growing up into Christ." Our destiny is not a world-hating one. The one in whom we are to grow up is one of us. We have, as Luther said, "a man in heaven." The Athanasian Creed puts it like this: God became one of us "not by conversion of the Godhead into flesh, but by taking of the Manhood into God."[4] God in Christ is available to us—now. Mae West might help us to understand the point a little if we reinterpret her famous line, "I'm no angel! Come up and see me sometime." Christ is no angel. He is our flesh and blood. The open invitation to all of us is to come up and see him, to grow up into him. Holy Week begins the ascent to the fullness of our humanity. It is the way home to our being more and more human.

Think of the story of Elijah. The question is not, Did it really happen? (although that *can* sometimes be important), but, Where does it touch and challenge me? I don't know whether Jesus *really* walked in water. Still less do I know whether Elijah *really* went up into heaven in a fiery chariot. What I do know is that our believing in God pulls out of us trust, obedience, and longing. Take an example from the New Testament (the story of Jesus walking on water). The key verse in the Gospel (Mark 6:45–52, RSV) is, "Take heart, it is I; have no fear." The point of the story of Elijah is that Elijah's God is to be trusted and is present in Elisha.

Another key verse in the Gospel is verse 52. Earlier the disciples had seen Jesus feed the five thousand. He now comes to them walking on water. The passage ends with the terrible words, "For they did not understand about the loaves, but their hearts were hardened." The disciples missed the point. The enemy is not doubting the literalness of the biblical stories. The enemy is "hardness of heart." The enemy is remaining closed to the fire and mystery inside us. Hardness of heart destroys our ability to become experiments in vulnerability. We are not open to forgiveness because, in our hardness, we believe that there is nothing to forgive.

The secret of life (which is the secret of Holy Week) is that life comes out of death. Learning to die is, therefore, the most important lesson we can learn. There is no growth without a kind of dying. Elisha saw Elijah taken up into heaven, and in his master's passing caught a glimpse of his own. "A grain of wheat, unless it fall into the ground and die, abideth alone" (John 12:24). On one of the earliest Christian tombstones we read, "We must die while we live, unless when we come to die we shall be dead indeed."

There are at least two ways to avoid the call to be experiments in vulnerability. We can avoid the wound of life. We can ignore the call to die in order to live. The first way is to claim it for ourselves. We take on the role of God, and when things don't go our way, we tend to say to ourselves such things as, "Let's bomb the hell out of them!" Isn't that why a person sometimes takes the law into his or her own hands? Doesn't such an attitude mar a government's foreign policy from time to time? Something breaks inside, and the otherwise friendly neighbor gets his shotgun and suddenly goes berserk. The second way is to give in to the temptation to feel satisfactorily helpless and hopeless! Like Clyde Gabriel, in *The Witches of Eastwick*, who murders his vicious, self-righteous wife:

Being in love with [his mistress] made Clyde drink more; drunk he could sink more relaxedly into the muck of longing. There was now an animal inside him whose gnawing was companionable, a kind of conversation. That he had once longed for his wife this way made his situation seem all the more satisfactorily hopeless. It was his misfortune to see through everything. He had not believed in God since he was seven, in patriotism since he was ten, in art since the age of fourteen, when he realized he would never be a Beethoven, a Picasso, or a Shakespeare. His favorite authors were the great seers-through—Nietzsche, Hume, Gibbon, the ruthless, jubilant lucid minds.

[But after the murder of his wife and the prelude to his suicide he] thought of the cozy basement and wondered whether, if he promised just to live there in one of the old coal bins and never go out doors, all might be forgiven and smoothed over.[5]

I find this a very moving passage and an accurate reading of the human heart—in its doubting, its pain, and its longing. The passion plays itself out in us whether we believe or not. The only difference between the believer and the unbeliever is that the former has learned to see and, therefore, will embrace the passion as his road to freedom and healing.

If we are to overcome our hardness of heart and respond to the fire and passion inside us, we have to learn to live gracefully with our fragility. James Hillman, a severe critic of the Judeo-Christian tradition, points to a fundamental maxim of the mystics, namely, that in order for a human being to be truly alive he has to come face to face with his greatest weakness. Acknowledging our weakness enables the soul to be born, and this birth requires the breakdown of the Western ego. This is a strange and dreadful-sounding requirement. As we have seen, Hillman claims that the soul is born anew precisely at the point when it experiences its own impotence. You happen, you become more your true self when you experience a kind of breakdown, a kind of death of the ego. When you cannot cope. "When you feel beaten, oppressed, knocked back... then something moves and you begin to feel yourself as a soul. You don't feel yourself as a soul when you're making it and doing it."⁶ This is alien to the popular way of thinking. The question we, who are concerned with the future of Christianity, must ask ourselves is, *What is it in our culture that furthers a sense of soul?* Hillman would insist that we first acknowledge that our reality is misshapen. Simply working on relationships, for example, won't do. Merely making up projects, even major ones, to service the ego or reorganize our world won't be able to meet the challenge of a distorted and distorting reality. If everything is bent out of shape and "the food is adulterated and the language you talk debased and the sounds mostly noise... the whole world is sick."⁷ There is no way that things can be put right by taking a course in better management either of one's soul or one's business because "it's not about meaning anymore; it's about survival."

I agree. The issue *is* survival. In order for us to survive we need to recover a sense of soul. At the moment we are in danger of living in a soulless (that is, lifeless) world. In Hillman's words, "we are living in a psychic concentration camp." And Christianity is partly responsible. What many of us who claim to be believers find hard to understand is that we are partly responsible for the age of terrorism in which we live. If we could own up to it perhaps things might change.

If you sit outside the Christian world, as an American Indian, as an Egyptian in the fourth century, as a Jew most anytime— Christianism looks pretty terrifying. Or just take the Japanese

*at Nagasaki; who brought them that bomb? Christianity has
a terrible shadow, and we have to begin somehow to take it
into ourselves.*[8]

Christianity easily degenerates into Christianism, and when it
does it casts an enormous and destructive shadow. Hillman uses
the state of Texas as a metaphor for Christianism, the disease that
is killing the soul, robbing it of its mystery and passion. Texas, for
him, is the symbol of a prevailing psychopathy that is as present in
New York and San Francisco as it is in Dallas. "Dallas… has the
highest divorce rate in America. Its teenage suicide rate is two and
a half times the national average. Ten thousand move here every
year; the Sun Belt, the golden crescent, it is for the young, rich,
determined, and powerful. It is not for the lost, the weak, and the
handicapped."[9]

The trouble is that the sickness is largely hidden. The psychopathy is invisible because, in the short term, our sickness of
soul pays off in material goods.

*Now I live in Texas. People don't worry there,… people don't
come apart, they just do it in the world and make money, too.
Shoot your father, shoot your son, rape, drink—the whole
family drinks—drive the car and drink, take this drug or that,
buy, buy, buy, change your face, lift your breasts, buy some
hair, different hair for different occasions. Put in a new heart.
Bypass the heart—what a metaphor! If you get tired of something, move out or sell or go bankrupt. Divorce it. If you want
it, marry it. Transvestites, transsexuals, trans-you-name-it. I
will name it: transcendence. There is something religious
underneath that makes them transcend all their conditions.
And this upward push pays off in economic success.*[10]

Our longing for transcendence gets corrupted, and our
hunger for God gets confused and identified with our greed for
material things. We get mired in "goods" even as we hunger for the
Good. We choke on the garbage we accumulate. Imagining that we

are fulfilling our dreams, we wonder why we are still hungry. Why doesn't the aching in the heart stop? Why won't the longing go away? It won't go away until we find out its true object.

We have confused our need to be truly earthed and rooted in the here and now with the accumulation and consumption of things.

> *When they use the word "development" in Dallas, they mean property... land-development... At the same time it's all church-backed. Fundamentalist. Do you see what I'm driving at? Psychopathic behavior is the fundamentalist behavior: taking fantasies literally and also confusing the literal and the concrete. Now this is just what the fundamentalist churches support: if your arm offend thee, cut it off. If your nose offend thee, get it straightened. Looking at a woman with lust is the same as doing it; doing it in the psyche and doing it in the street become identical. If they say "tuck in your belly," they go out and take a tuck in it, surgically. If you need a lift, you get a face-lift. The metaphors become utterly concrete...*[11]

Sometimes our pathology gets the better of us, and we break out into acts of violence or depravity. At other times we live in "a kind of Muzak blankness, out of which pop moments of sentiment or some new idea of making money." The corporation mind has taken over our souls and answers our deepest longings from the point of view of "economics." When economics replaces moral commitment we have already given in to the sickness eating at our souls.

There's no doubt that Hillman has allowed his frustration and anger to distort his vision. He does, however, hit where it hurts and for that reason is worth attending to. We are challenged with the issue of "soul," the issue of transcendence. How am I going to die? How am I going to live? Where is my "soul?" Elijah was taken up by a whirlwind. What or who takes you up? Our whirlwind is Christ—to take you up, out of yourself, and form a deeper "you."

No wonder Christianity is best described as a love story. God has fallen in love with you and wants you to come home. What greater force is there on earth for transformation and change than love? It continually takes us by surprise.

When it comes, will it come without warning

Just as I'm picking my nose?
Will it knock at my door in the morning,
Or tread in the bus on my toes?
Will it come like a change in the weather?
Will its greeting be courteous or rough?
Will it alter my life altogether?
O tell me the truth about love.[12]

The love of Holy Week is a whirlwind of life-altering passion that you can ignore or accept. The choice is yours. If you want to see just how far God has fallen in love with you, then look at Jesus—look at Jesus on the cross. I shrink back, because I would rather have a kind of second-class loving, over which I had some control, than this passionate whirlwind. But I do not know of any other way home. It is the only way I know that brings me, not only home to God, but home to myself and to you. Our place of meeting is in the heart of God, and during this week it is the scene of hurt and conflict. I cannot get home without allowing myself to be taken up by the One who died on the cross.

STUDY QUESTIONS

1. Jones tells of his own commitment to "a ruthlessly honest exercise of memory" (p. 113). What is the promise in being thus committed? What costs does it carry?

2. Abraham Heschel is quoted as suggesting that there are two kinds of ignorance: "One is insipid, caused by negligence, oversight; the other lucid, the result of diligence, insight. The one leads to vanity and complacency; the other to humility and understanding" (p. 115). How are we to discern between the two kinds? What responses are called for?

3. What are the three things with which Christianity tends to be identified? (See p. 117.) With what other things might Christianity rightly be identified to round out the mystery? "How do you know the genuine article?"

4. Jones writes, "We have confused our need to be truly earthed and rooted in the here and now with the accumulation and consumption of things" (p. 123). What tools do you find useful in striking the balance between the transcendent and the concrete? How do you recognize healthy groundedness in others?

10.
WHO IS THAT MAN NAILED TO THOSE TWO PIECES OF WOOD?

"Who is that man nailed to those pieces of wood, Mommy?" asked the child of a friend of mine. They were looking at a crucifix, and it shocked my friend that her child was unaware of who Jesus was. The shock, I suspect, did not, in the first instance, spring from a fear for the child's soul but rather from a realization that her son was growing up entirely ignorant of one of the wellsprings of Western civilization. To grow up without knowing who Jesus Christ was and to remain ignorant of the religion that bears his name spoke of a devastating cultural deprivation. The mother's shock was cultural and aesthetic. Her realization of her child's ignorance startled her sufficiently to ask fundamental questions about who she was and what kind of society she lived in. It revived in her the conviction that she was a pilgrim and a pilgrim who was meant for joy.

Underneath all cultural and aesthetic questions there lurks basic religious ones of Who am I? Who are you? Who are we? Why are we here? Where are we going? The artistic endeavors of men and women are, in part, attempts to respond to, or rage at, those dark and powerful questions. They push us into unasked-for areas of exploration.

On the wall in the south transept of Grace Cathedral, San Francisco, is a large and impressive Romanesque crucifix. It is beautiful, compelling, and moving. Who is that man nailed to those pieces of wood? I find it painful to reflect that many children and scores of adults do not even know who he is. We live in a culture where children are growing up ignorant of the name of Jesus—except as a swearword. Traditionally, Jesus is the name behind all our individual names and our attempt to name things and people. The name of Jesus frees us to say "I am" and "We are" in a new way. How is this so?

In order to answer the question, How so? we have to be prepared to ask the most probing question of all. When we ask, Who is Jesus? another question, closer to home, is posed at the depths of our being: Who are you asking the question? If we are willing to *look* at Jesus long enough (and I invite you to take a long hard and loving look at the image of the crucified God), the question of our own identity is disturbingly posed. It can, of course, be easily dismissed. It is, however, part of the vocation of the Church to be both an inspiration and an irritant to keep the question alive: in its liturgy, its music, and its preaching. That is why the Church is important. It goads us into pilgrimage and supports us on our journey.

The silent and broken man on the cross looks out at us and asks, "Who *are* you? *Who* are you? Who are *you*? Pictures of love and suffering do this to us. If we are open to them, they, in turn, open us up. It used to be a jibe that people only come to church to be seen. There's a sense in which this is fundamentally true. Coming to church is a form of exposure, a nakedness before God. We do come to church to be seen, but not so much by others as by God. Worship is our great unmasking for the asking of the Great Questions.

In the Bible we find these questions raised in the humanizing and stretching contradictions of the gospel. We are invited to search the Scriptures and seek the mind of Christ so that we can find out who we are. Yet my mind is far from Christlike. In fact, my mind resists being formed by one who was "content" to be crucified. My mind has better things to do. It is full of other things. My Judas-mind suffers from a sense of outrage that God doesn't do a better job of running the world! In one of Woody Allen's films, God is referred to as "an underachiever"! On the face of it, as I gaze at the crucifix, God appears to have failed. My fear and vindictiveness come together when I think of the virulence of terrorism and fanaticism of (for example) fundamentalist forms of the great religions. Ivan Karamazov was right. Religion is a menace.

Religion (as "secular humanists" would have us believe) has done more harm than good in the world. We are all better off without it. We live in a world where the taking of hostages and wanton and gratuitous acts of murder have become routine. What possible difference could "the mind of Christ" make? Frankly, it makes little difference unless we are willing to be formed by it. We, in Christ, can and do make a difference. That is what the Passion is about. The secularist critique of religion has merit with regard to some of its practitioners, but secularism's great flaws are its naive faith in human reason (surely terminally discredited both by the advances in psychology and psychiatry in this century and by the history of the recent past) and its misreading of the human heart. Humanism without God is passionless. It is an inhuman humanism. The reason for human woe is the lack of true religion, not its popularity.

"Who is that man nailed to those pieces of wood, Mommy?" The world in which we live raises questions about us and our basic approach to life (whether we are believers or not): do we have a vision of life that stretches us, fools us out of our limits, and continually invites us to ask the Great Questions? Or do we stifle the spirit and opt for a set of ready-made answers? Some of our children are already suffering from a view of education that would eliminate questioning altogether. Education, it is believed, is about answers, clear and unequivocal—it should not be concerned with questions. So runs the argument of those school districts that ban books and are fearful of wonder, fantasy, and questioning. This spirit also infects the churches. Religion is for the solving of questions rather than for keeping them alive. For my part I would rather have us struggle with the question of who Jesus is and who we are than have us come up with easy, idolatrous answers. Easy answers to hard questions dull the mind and deaden the spirit. I am not talking about wallowing in doubt and uncertainty, as if floundering for its own sake were a virtue. The issue here is concerned with the way the Spirit of God enlivens us when we are willing to ask the same questions again and again from deeper and deeper places in the human heart. Who is that man nailed to the cross?

When I am willing to ask the question with a full heart, two things are uncovered in myself: my rebelliousness and my weakness. St. Paul, in 2 Cor. 12:2–10, glories in his weakness. There's not doubt about our weakness either, although few of us find it an occasion of glory. The Bible, in pointing to our rebelliousness and weakness, extends to us an extraordinary invitation. In order to be fully alive and to grow we need to be in touch with our rebelliousness and hostility, on the one hand, and with our amazing fragility as human beings, on the other. When I look at Jesus and ask, "Who is that man?" I come face to face with both my rebelliousness and weakness, with both my outrage and my impotence. No wonder I "fall foul" or Jesus, just as his first hearers did. In Mark 6:1–6 we find Jesus among his own people. Their response is, "Where does he get it from? Who does he think he is?" Just as Jesus fell foul of the people in the synagogue, so he falls foul of all of us today. Jesus is particularly scathing with regard to those who fancy that they are "religious." This seems to be the inevitable fate of those who struggle with the truth and dare try to articulate it. No one in his or her right mind wants to be stripped naked and asked terrible questions. The crucified man, in exposing my rebelliousness and weakness, pushes me out into the unknown.

Let us look a little more closely at the Bible, which continually poses the questions. The prophet Ezekiel, for example (2:1–7), was sent to a rebellious people. They were politically selfish, stubborn, and obstinate. They were blind to the truth of their situation. They were like us. We know very well that we are "not unlucky but evil"! In this terrible insight, rebellion and weakness come together. As we saw earlier, it takes a great deal of spiritual maturity to acknowledge our own capacity for evil, to admit there is no act, however revolting, of which we would not be capable under certain circumstances. In the middle of this rebellion and weakness, God in Christ invites us into dialogue. It is through this conversation we begin to find out who we really are. God said to Ezekiel, "Son of man, stand up upon thy feet! Let me talk with you." In the midst of our rebellion and weakness God speaks to us. God speaks to us in the form of a broken and ruined man on a cross.

A great deal of harm can be done in the name of religion by people who are not in touch with their own fragility. Religion can be a terrible weapon in the hands of the frightened and unsure. People have been hurt by men and women who thought God was speaking to them. Some, to be sure, did and do a great deal of good based on this conviction, but it is easy to see how religious people sometimes get blown up with self-importance when they imagine that they have received a special word from Almighty God. This is part of the tragic weakness of much TV evangelism. The preacher has a "hot line" to God, but there seems to be no means of verifying the connection! Some forms of popular Christianity have been so harmful as to be the occasion of the founding of an organization known as "Fundamentalists Anonymous," which is based on the twelve-step programs that deal with alcohol and drug addiction. Religion that is not in touch with the aching and the hoping at the center of the human heart can easily lead to a form of craziness. There is no deeper and more harmful craziness than the kind that thinks it can control the passionate Whirlwind we call God.

St. Paul was well aware of the dangers of being puffed up by religious experience. He knew about the dangerous craziness that accompanies it. Paul glories in his weakness and refuses to base his authority on any special esoteric experience. His one great experience on the road to Damascus blinded him and sent him on a humbling inner journey to prepare him for his mission. The encounter with Jesus put Paul's whole being into question and pushed him into pilgrimage. The upheaval was so great that he had to be given a new name. Saul became Paul.

When I am inflated or deflated, when I am possessed by arrogance or by the conviction of my own insignificance, I am a slave, unfree, shackled by an ego that knows how to be the center of its own attention. "How important I am!" I say to myself, or, "How unimportant I am!" Both are traps that hide me from you and from myself. Both freeze me into immobility. There is no pilgrimage. There is no need for one. I find myself in an illusory world. Our way back to reality is to learn to distrust our view of things. We hardly know how to experience the world with any degree of accuracy. We are seduced by a false view filtered through our addictions, fears, and greeds. These addictions, fears, and greeds are part of what Paul means by "weakness." Then there are the limitations of personality, physical conditions, and circumstances. These also we sometimes experience as "weakness." All the great religious traditions invite us to distrust our experience, to ask radical and disturbing questions so that our horizons may be widened. Such questioning will bring us to the end of our rope, to *the* question for which there is no answer except our surrender to the love of God, which invites us simply to say Yes!

"If you meet the Buddha on the road, kill him!"—so runs the ancient dictum. If you think you've got the answer, then look again. Or, as St. Augustine, put it, "If you have understood, then what you have understood is not God!" In secular terms, we might way, "If you have understood, you have not yet been fully informed." It is said that St. Teresa of Avila, when one of her nuns told her that she had just seen a vision of the Blessed Virgin Mary, replied, "Never mind, dear, it will go away!" And St. Philip Neri (one of the most humane and loving saints) told one of his followers who had had a similar vision, "Next time she appears, spit in her eye!" When he did so, it is said, the devil appeared. All these stories remind us of the fragility and unreliability of our interpretation of reality. That is why we need each other. I need you to help me test what I think I know of God, of the world, of others. What we *say* about reality matters. Words matter. They have power to reveal and to hide, to build up or drag down, to heal or to hurt.

Words tell us who we are. Those who have power over our words about ourselves and our world have power over us. That is why politics, religion, and sex have been taboo subjects in so-called polite circles. The words explode, and people get hurt. Words lie as well as tell the truth—especially in these three areas: politics, sex, and religion. In the supermarket of ideologies, in the psychic dark pool in which we all swim, we are invited to stand before the cross of Christ in silence and wait, wait for the din of ideology to die down, wait for the water to clear so that we can both hear and see the Word who tells us who we are and what we are about. That Word is Jesus. He is God's Word to me about myself. He and only he is the one who defines me and in him I am freed from all the definitions that politics, sexuality, and religion (as ideology) would impose upon me.

We can think of other examples of brutally narrowing self-definition besides sexuality. What word defines you? Who or what says who you are? How do you measure success? Look at us as a nation hoping for a liberating word to tell us that we are all right. We are the most powerful nation in the world, yet our foreign policy is in disarray, our commitments to our own safety at all costs is suicidal. There is a lot of random and damaging ideology that defines us as a people. Whatever defines us, enslaves us—our sexuality, our color, our pedigree—unless it is placed in the context of our identity in God.

Holy Week and the Drama of the Passion break us open by inviting us to see ourselves in the light of Christ and so be free men and women. The "Word" that defines us is Christ, not "words" taken from politics, ideology, or sexuality.

God says, "I fell in love with you from your very beginning, and I want you to come home. Let me talk with you! Let me rescue you from the narrowing spiral of your self-definitions." To move away from that narrow world is to journey toward heaven where, as Dante observed, we are able to shine back to God with the splendor of the divine light and say, "I am!" Who is that man on the cross? He is the One who enables you to say with full voice, I am!

A human being is, therefore, one who enters into a conversation with God. It is this Word of God and Word from God that constitutes us, making us who we are. No one but God (thank God) can truly tell me who I am. This is what the Church means when it says over and over again, "Repent and believe. Be born again." The Word that defines us is Jesus and no one and nothing else. Jesus is God's Word to me about myself, about you, and about our world.

What does that mean? God's Passion, as remembered and celebrated in Holy Week, is an annual reminder of this ever-expanding horizon of self-definition. The Passion story serves as an inspiration and an irritant. As pilgrims, we define ourselves as people related to a limitless horizon and to an unpredictable future. Thus, it is to place ourselves in the hands of God. No wonder St. Paul was aware of his "weakness," and no wonder Jesus was rejected by his own people. Who can tolerate such liberty? What we rebel against is the terrible freedom of a limitless horizon. The Grand Inquisitor had compassion on the ant heap of the human race that could not possibly bear the burden of true freedom.

"Who is that man nailed to those pieces of wood, Mommy?" Being willing to ask that question in new and disturbing ways is already to be on pilgrimage. The answer to the question provides the key to our saying "I am" and "We are" in new and unimagined ways. The way we say or learn to say these simple words determines the future of the world. In them, we either choose life or death. Jesus, the Word of God, is here, now in the persons of our brothers and sisters. The bread of life is consecrated on Christian altars throughout the world every day. Sunday by Sunday, day by day. At the altar, a rebellious yet fragile people is invited to find a new identity, a new way of being in the world and with each other so that we will live and not die. The secret of who you really are is available to you, even in your resistance and rebellion, even in your weakness and powerlessness. God is in love with Judas and Ivan as much as with anyone else. The saving Word of love is Jesus. Jesus. Jesus. The man on the cross says, "I have always been in love with you! Come home! Come and *look*. Come and *taste*. Come and be *free*."

Who is that man nailed to those two pieces of wood? Your answer to that question will determine who you are. It is now time to come to Calvary and wait at the foot of the cross, not only to see what happens, but to allow time for you to happen in a new way.

STUDY QUESTIONS

1. Who in your life might ask the question, "Who is that man nailed to those two pieces of wood?" How would you respond? What would happen if you were to speak of Jesus before they asked? Try it.

2. Jones asks, "do we have a vision of life that stretches us, fools us out of our limits, and continually invites us to ask the Great Questions?" (p. 128). How do you respond? What would such a vision look like? What about it is particularly inviting to you?

3. Jones writes, "Religion that is not in touch with the aching and the hoping at the center of the human heart can easily lead to a form of craziness" (p. 130). This aching and hoping keep us from a self-centered immobility. "Our way back to reality is to learn distrust our view of things" (p. 130). How do you respond to the call to "distrust our experience"? What reasons does Jones offer for doing so? How do you sense the movement of the Spirit within you?

4. In a world of words, Jones invites us to "stand before the cross of Christ in silence and wait, wait for the din of ideology to die down, wait for the water to clear so that we can both hear and see the Word who tells us who we are and what we are about" (p. 131). When in your life do you wait? Is waiting comfortable? What happens when you wait in stillness before God?

11.
THE TREE JOINING HEAVEN
AND EARTH

Author of the World's Joy,
Bearer of the World's Pain,
At the heart of all our distress
Let unconquerable gladness dwell.

Our journey has been so that "broken bones may joy." But the joy
that is real cannot and must not suppress its knowledge of the
world's pain. In Norse mythology there is an ash tree (Yggdrasil)
joining heaven and earth. Its roots and branches bind together
heaven, earth, and hell. One side of the tree is dead. The other side
is vibrant with life. It is our task to climb around the trunk of the
tree. Sometimes we find ourselves on the living side; at other times
on the dead. It is all one tree. Reading the story of Christ's Passion
and Crucifixion, one cannot help but see the parallel between
Yggdrasil and the cross. Believers through the ages have seen the
cross as the Tree of Life, binding together heaven, earth, and hell.

The Christian religion makes an extraordinary claim about
this tree. Because of the cross of Jesus everything is different. What
kind of difference do the Passion and death and Resurrection of
Jesus make? Jesus has made all the difference to my life, and, as
inadequate as words are, I want to try to say how. Not long ago the
American people had the opportunity to watch an ongoing
national soap opera in the form of the Iran-Contra hearings. My
own involvement in listening to the questioning surprised me by
its intensity. It wasn't so much that I was caught up in the question
of the morality of covert practices as with the effort on the part of
Congress to get at the truth. The pages and pages of testimonial
seemed, in a Kafkaesque way, to muddy the waters rather than
clarify them. An image kept coming to my mind and would not go
away. I saw myself sitting in the witness box, surrounded by piles

of papers (the testimony of my life). The prosecution lawyer was relentlessly questioning me about the minutest details of my life. I found myself sweating—trying to remember the details, trying to justify not simply my actions on any given occasion but also my whole life, my "me." To make matters worse, my judges were both blind and deaf!

I think that image speaks to a perennial human disease. We are all in the business of self-justification. Jesus makes all the difference in my life, because through faith in him I am taken out of the courtroom into a totally different environment. I am welcomed into a household were I belong and am loved. I don't know how it happens exactly except that as long as I have been on pilgrimage to and with Jesus Christ crucified I have experienced my life, with all its ups and downs, as a Way of Liberation. In Jesus, I am beginning to come "home" to myself. St. Paul in his letter to the Romans describes this homecoming: "The conclusion of the matter is this: there is no condemnation for those who are united with Christ Jesus, because in Christ Jesus the life-giving law of the Spirit has set you free from the law of sin and death" (Rom. 8:1, NEB).

It would be a mistake, however, to think that my troubles are over. There is much that I do not understand. Judas Iscariot and Ivan Karamazov are still my soul mates. I have now come to accept them as my brothers. They no longer have the hold over me they once had, but they are always with me. They, too, need loving out of their disappointment, cynicism, and despair. My homecoming in Christ does not release me from the necessity of having to face the consequences for my actions. I still feel the sting of my betrayals and am made numb by things I cannot accept, but I can now face them from within the household of the lovers of God. And that makes all the difference.

There is a montage in which the artist John Heartfield has taken a rather bland painting of Christ carrying the cross (by the Danish artist Thorwaldsen) and has added to it a Nazi functionary screwing four extra pieces of wood at right angles to it so as to make a swastika. The montage is subtitled, "The crucifix was not yet heavy enough." Judas and Ivan point to the various ways in which the cross has been made into a swastika or its equivalent. They will not let me avert my eyes. Good Friday is *the* day of days on which I am invited to look into the heart of the mystery of God's passionate love for me.

Good Friday is the day of days when we see the collision of two passions—our passion for God and God's Passion for us. From this collision of two longings, a light so bright that one cannot look directly at it is generated. My companions, Judas and Ivan, tell me that my "God" is in pieces and my religion in a shambles. Good Friday, far from being *good*, is a day of failure and disappointment. At best the cross is a flop; at worst a hoax. The cross is surely the rock of atheism, yet believers find it the rock of faith. The believer and the unbeliever find themselves on the same rock. Judas and Ivan look at me with a sad satisfaction and say, "I told you so!" I look back and have nothing to say except, "Wait!" The cross *is* the rock of faith, but faith in a God we can scarcely imagine, let alone understand. *If* we want to understand a little of the mystery of the Passion we must be content to wait at the foot of the cross. That in itself can be hard work. Our culture is not sympathetic to waiting and watching by the dying and the dead.

First, we wait at the foot of the cross to listen to what it says to us mythically. I mean this in the best sense of the word *myth*. How does the myth of the Yggdrasil tree help me understand something of the mystery of the cross? It tells me that something *more* might be going on here than a first-century execution in an unattractive outpost of the Roman Empire. The cross might be a cosmic event. The cross, like Yggdrasil, is the *axis mundi*, the axis of the world. It joins heaven and earth and around it the whole of reality revolves. In traditional Christian mythology the cross is set up in the exact place where there once grew the Tree of Life in the Garden of Eden. The cross is a new Tree of Life set up in what is destined to be a New Garden. The cross brings us home to paradise. In many pictures of the Crucifixion we find a skull at its base. It is the skull of Adam. The new tree of the New Adam is planted on the grave of the Old Adam and the old tree. All of this is worthy of our attention. If we are willing to wait and watch, the imagery could cause a revolution in our own self-understanding. We could, as millions of others have in the past, experience something of the healing power of the cross to reinterpret our lives... "There is no condemnation...!" A new beginning was made here on Calvary, and that new beginning changed the meaning of history and enables you and me to come home.

Ivan whispers in my ear, "This may be very well from the point of view of mythology. I am even able to admit that there is much food for thought and even prayer. But what about the real world of real pain? For heaven's sake, come down to earth!" I wonder if it is possible to say anything about human suffering that doesn't sound hollow, that won't cause Ivan to insist on returning his ticket?

The novelist and poet Robert Graves returned home on leave as a second lieutenant during the First World War. It was Holy Week, and he went to church on Good Friday 1916. The preacher talked about suffering in such a way that Graves, who had seen the horrors of trench warfare, never went to church again. Graves returned his ticket. He wanted no part of the Christian charade. This vignette in the life of one man on Good Friday 1916 is in direct contrast with another story about Good Friday 1945. The incident is set in the Ravensbruck concentration camp where 92,000 women and children died. Imagine a group of women lined up for the gas chamber. It is Good Friday. One of them becomes hysterical. From the crowd of other women not chosen for death that day a figure emerges and approaches the woman broken by fear and hysteria and says, "It's all right. It's all right. I'll take your place." That woman was Elizabeth Pilenko. She came from a wealthy land-owning family in the south of Russia and eventually became a nun and worked among the poor. During the war the convent became a haven for Jews. When the Gestapo came to the convent, Mother Maria (as Elizabeth Pilenko was called) was arrested and sent to Ravensbruck. There she made a lasting impression, and even the guards spoke of her as "that wonderful Russian nun." I do not understand how one human being can go up to another who is condemned to die and say, "Don't be frightened. Look, I shall take your turn." In line with the rest, Mother

Maria entered the gas chamber. I do not understand it, yet I am deeply disturbed and moved by it. When I allow myself to think about it and to acknowledge my feelings, something powerful stirs within me that makes me feel both ashamed and hopeful: ashamed because of the lack of passion and concern in my own life; hopeful that there is a love that can inspire human beings to go beyond that which is "reasonable." With acts like that of Mother Maria, life is catapulted into a higher and wider orbit. How I long to be her companion! How I dread the possibility!

The "unreasonableness of love" is expressed in a prayer that the soldiers who liberated the death camp found near the body of a dead child and written on a piece of wrapping paper.

O Lord,
remember not only the men and women of goodwill
but also those of ill will.
But do not remember the suffering they have
inflicted on us.
Remember the fruits we brought to this suffering,
our comradeship, our loyalty, our humility,
the courage, the generosity,
the greatness of heart which has grown out of all
this.
And when they come to judgement,
let all the fruits that we have borne
be their forgiveness. Amen.

Two particular phrases touch me at the depths. The first is, "Remember… the greatness of heart which has grown out of all this." The promise is that out of a great passion can come the kind of greatness of heart displayed in Mother Maria. The second: "And when they"—the bad, the cruel, the indifferent, you and I—"come to judgement, let all the fruits that we have borne be their forgiveness." It this how redeeming love works? Is it possible that suffering, willingly undertaken for the sake of love, can be poured into a crucible of passion and be transformed into an elixir that brings healing and forgiveness to others? Could I make that much difference? Good Friday invites me to revolutionize my thinking and open my heart.

When I think about Mother Maria saying, "Look, I shall take your place," or read the prayer written on a scrap of paper by an unknown victim, I find that I experience the painful emergence of meaning in a meaningless world. At first, the meaning that struggles to manifest itself is terrible in that all it does is to give shape to the suffering of the world. What emerges is the vision of the world as a crucifix. This terrible truth gives meaning of sorts to our lives. St. Bonaventure, writing in *The Tree of Life*, suggests that as Jesus was thrown roughly upon the wood of the cross, spread out, pulled forward, stretched back and forth like a hide, so humanity is pierced by pointed nails and fixed to the cross. The fact that it happened to Jesus becomes a sign for the meaning of suffering in the world. I don't understand it. I don't like it. But the Ivan Karamazov within me isn't so sure that he wants to return his ticket.

I move out from the painful cynicism of a Robert Graves to the passion of another soldier in that same war. G. A. Studdert Kennedy, like St. Bonaventure before him, saw not meaninglessness but humanity itself nailed to the cross. Studdert Kennedy recalls that on June 7, 1917, he found himself on the wrong side of the line of battle. During heavy shelling and half mad with fear, he ran in the direction of the British lines. As he stumbled through what had once been a wooded copse, he fell over something. "I stopped to see what it was. It was an undersized, underfed German boy, with a wound in his stomach and a hole in his head. I remember muttering, 'You poor little devil, what had you got to do with it?'" It was then that the terrible illumination came. It seemed to Studdert Kennedy that the boy disappeared and there in his place lay the Christ on the cross who cried, "Inasmuch as ye have done it unto the least of these my little ones ye have done it unto me." "From that moment on," he records, "I never saw a battlefield as anything but a crucifix. From that moment on I have never seen the world as anything but a crucifix."

How "reasonable" is it to claim that a cruciform world is a world full of meaning? I believe there is meaning here simply because it is part of a love story, a Passion Play. The story *can* help us bear the reality in which we find ourselves. The drama *can* illuminate the drama in which we are often unwilling actors. There is not one of us who does not carry a scar or two from this Passion. There is no one who has not played a part, however small, in this drama. We all carry the wounds of our loving and our hating, of our hoping and our despairing. Are any of us free of scars? Can we hope to enter fully into our pilgrimage without the necessity of further wounding? In a powerful poem, Amy Carmichael speaks to my dread:

> *Hast thou no scar?*
> *No hidden scar on foot, or side, or hand?*
> *I hear thee sung as mighty in the land,*
> *I hear them hail thy bright ascendent star:*
> *Hast thou no scar?*
>
> *Hast thou no wound?*
> *Yet, I was wounded by the archers, spent,*
> *Leaned me against the tree to die, and rent*
> *By ravening beasts that compassed me, I swooned:*
> *Hast thou no wound?*
>
> *No wound? No scar?*
> *Yes, as the master shall the servant be,*
> *And pierced are the feet that follow me;*
> *But thine are whole. Can he have followed far*
> *Who has no wound? No scar?*[1]

I still use a great deal of my energy in trying to domesticate suffering and my numb fear of it. I would like my pilgrimage to be contained in a kind of adventure park of the Spirit, Disneyland of the Holy Ghost. I would like the thrill of facing simulated dangers and the comfort of living in a kind of "Heritage Village" of the soul. I would prefer mechanized villains and prefabricated terrors in the hope that I might short-circuit the work of this larger

Passion playing itself out in the world. The trouble is that it keeps breaking in. To be human, to be fully human is to enter into the mystery of real suffering. To acknowledge that simple fact is to begin not only to understand the possible meaning of suffering but also to share in that suffering that is God's Passion. The world *is* a crucifix, but it is God's crucifix. The pilgrim's path leads from human suffering to God's Passion. For Christianity to be worth believing, nothing must be left out of the story. On Good Friday we are given an account of the darkest and the worst that this world offers its children. A tree is set up between heaven and earth. Its branches touch heaven. Its roots are in hell. Nothing and no one is left out.

In the end the Crucifixion is not a spectator sport. I cannot simply watch on the sidelines. Something bursts within me— revulsion, hatred, disappointment—but I am not left untouched. The cross, acknowledged or not, leaves its own kind of wound in us. It sets us voyaging inside ourselves. The world is a crucifix. The world is a tree. Its knotty entrails contain all my hatreds; its leafy branches, all my hopes. My homecoming is dependent on its loving purpose. Marcos Ana, who spent twenty-two years as a political prisoner in Burgos Jail, wrote,

> *Listen now, whoever you may be,*
> *if your soul is lit by the love of God:*
> *you cannot leave the world all by yourself,*
> *set out on the great path with empty hands,*
> *arrive before the Gates of God—which your faith dreams*
> *stand underneath the arch of the Eternal Home—*
> *to say, "Lord, Lord, I have brought nothing with me;*
> *give me a place of love in your divine light."*
> *Because the Lord your God will answer "Go.*
> *Hack up your feet on red unending ice,*
> *lean on the knotted stick of all your hatreds;*
> *and you shall wander eternally unless*
> *you find the palm of love which you refused to take*
> *from the tree which was seeded by my blood."*[2]

Hatred of God may bring the soul to God. There are countless witnesses who can testify that at Calvary they found the strangest of gods and the deepest of lovers. God is a lover who is so vulnerable that he is broken for us, so weak that he needs protection from us. There is a scene in Frederick Buechner's novel, *Brendan*, where a blind man, Mahon, teaches the monk how to play chess. Brendan relates all the pieces and the moves they make to the Christian pilgrimage.

Save for pawns, Mahon said, the king was weakest of all. He could move any way he wished but only a step at a time. Yet he was the dearest piece even so, Mahon said, for the whole game hung on keeping him safe. Brendan told him Christ too is just such a king in his weakness, meek and lowly of heart and like a sheep dumb before its shearers. It's ourselves above all we must keep him safe from, Brendan said, for with our dark ways we're ever bringing woe upon him.[3]

The God on the cross needs to be kept safe from the woe our hatreds wreak upon his body. And we are God's body. The Judas figure in me rages. What are all my betrayals next to "how God betrays this bleeding world for sport each bleeding bloody day?... Thou holy bleeding God... I piss for spite into your lovely eyes."[4] Thus it is by the grace flowing from the pens of writers (like Frederick Buechner), who know that anatomy of the soul, that I am able to find my own rage and dare spew it out in a terrible prayer. My rage at the cross is turned into wonder; my hatred into tears of joy, because I begin to realize that God *knows*, really knows, what it is to suffer. In God's agony is mirrored the struggle of my own soul. God and I, God and all of us, are together on the cross. It is a great tree that binds everything together.

I am not given to tears, so that when I do cry it is particularly significant. Over twenty-five years ago I read Helen Waddell's *Peter Abelard*. I ended up crying in my room in college. One particular incident near the end of the book triggered it. Abelard, who had suffered terrible misfortunes, is walking in the woods with his friend Thibault. They hear a piercing cry of pain. They run and find a rabbit caught in a trap. "O God, let it die. Let it die quickly." Thibault releases it from the trap and Abelard holds the wounded creature in his arms, where it dies.

It was that last confiding thrust that broke Abelard's heart. He looked down at the little draggled body, his mouth shaking. "Thibault," he said, "do you think there is a God at all? Whatever has come to me, I earned it. But what did this one do?"

Thibault nodded.

"I know," he said. "Only—I think God is in it too."

Abelard looked up sharply.

"In it? Do you mean that it makes Him suffer, the way it does us?"

Again Thibault nodded.

"Then why doesn't He stop it?"

"I don't know," said Thibault. "Unless—unless it's like the Prodigal Son. I suppose the father could have kept him at home against his will. But what would have been the use? All this," he stroked the limp body, "is because of us. But all the time God suffers. More than we do."

Abelard looked perplexed... "Thibault, do you mean Calvary?" Thibault shook his head. "That was only a part of it—the piece that we saw—in time. Like that." He pointed to a fallen tree beside them, sawn through the middle. "That dark ring there, it goes up and down the whole length of the tree. But you see only where it is cut across. That is what Christ's life was; the bit of God that we saw. And we think God is like that, because Christ was like that, kind and forgiving sins and healing people. We think God is like that forever, because it happened once, with Christ. But not the pain. Not the agony at last. We think that stopped."...

"Then, Thibault," [Abelard] said slowly, "you think that all this... all the pain of the world, was Christ's cross?"

"God's cross," said Thibault. "And it goes on."

"The Patripassian heresy," muttered Abelard mechani-

cally. "But, O God, if it were true. Thibault it must be. At least, there is something at the back of it that is true. And if we could find it—it would bring back the whole world."[5]

In the death of the rabbit, Abelard caught a glimpse of the God of pathos. For a moment he let go of his conception of the God of classical theism and saw something of the God who suffers. His automatic reaction, "the Patripassian heresy" (literally, the doctrine of God the Father suffering) gave way to a more spontaneous response. An apathetic God is hardly a God at all. Such a God, unmoved by the suffering of the world, would be Ivan's God. We would have good reason to return our ticket.

When I am willing to see the cross as God's, the Judas, the Ivan within me begins to weep. I move from the vision of pointless suffering in the world to a vision of God's Passion. The believer is one who is moved by the pathos of God in such a way that his or her whole life is turned around. It is God's suffering love that brings us home. God's Passion is a victory of love, the purpose of which is to bring the whole world home. That is why Good Friday is called good. It is the Day of the Great Tree, joining heaven and earth.

Author of the World's Joy,
Bearer of the World's Pain,
At the heart of all our distress
Let unconquerable gladness dwell.

Study Questions

1. Jones writes of the "perennial human disease" of self-justification (p. 136). Where in your life do you feel called on to justify yourself? Where do you ask others for their self-justification? Where are you welcomed that you belong and are loved?

2. In speaking of the new beginning that was made on Calvary, Jones suggests that "There is no condemnation...!" after the healing power of the cross reinterprets our lives. What does this evoke in you? How does this idea relate to traditional doctrine?

3. Jones states, "To be human, to be fully human is to enter into the mystery of real suffering," and "For Christianity to be worth believing, nothing must be left out of the story" (p. 142). What parts of our society would need to change to accept this truth? What parts of your own life?

4. Jones quotes Helen Waddell's *Peter Abelard* as a particularly powerful book in his life. In the story, Thibault compares the pain of God to the ring of a tree, visible only in a particular place, but running up and down the full length of the tree (p. 144). What comes up in you as you reflect on the pervasiveness of God's pain? What changes does Jones describe in his own awareness?

III.
THE CALL TO GLORY

12.
EASTER IS NOW!

Easter has largely deteriorated into a secular festival celebrating the coming of spring. At best, it celebrates the cycle of the seasons. At worst, it provides us with yet another occasion to spend money. Either way, the "glory" it celebrates can be pretty thin. My memories of Easter are of chocolate, eggs, and flowers. But, as W. S. Gilbert wrote, "The flowers that bloom in the Spring, tra-la, have nothing to do with the case." Easter is not the celebration of the coming of spring. If Easter is not a flower festival, then what is it? Did Jesus rise from the dead, and if he did, what difference does it make?

The question, Did it really happen? is bound to be central to the celebration of Easter. But it is a very hard one for modern people to answer. What is the "it" that is supposed to have happened? The Church proclaims that Jesus was raised on the third day. This I believe with all my heart. Merely believing such a fantastic event as if it were reported on the late news wouldn't really make that much difference to our lives. No doubt, we'd be impressed and soon our attention would move on to something else. Our consciousness is formed and deformed by the media, which crunch the reporting of all events to fit an attention span of about thirty seconds. The media are interested only in "events" that can be recorded, photographed, circulated, and forgotten. So, when we ask, Did the resurrection happen? we expect it to have been like something on the CBS news. Imagine a first-century "anchor man": "Early this morning, Jesus of Nazareth was raised from the dead. His disciples are nowhere to be found and the authorities are looking into the matter. Now for other items in the news. The emperor has sent two legions to the northern provinces. The price of corn rose, and there is trouble in North Africa." The "news" hardly touches us. There is really nothing new about it. Our problem is that we wouldn't know a world-changing event even if we saw one. We don't know how to *look* at things. The news camera is like the eye of an unblinking toad. It records everything and understands nothing. The Resurrection changed the world, and such an event is resistant to cameras and tape recorders. It takes something quite different. Our pilgrimage has been a long exercise in preparing our vision so that we might be able to see the healing power of the radically new.

No one, as far as we know, actually saw the Resurrection take place, and very few actually encountered the risen Christ. There were chosen witnesses, and because the Resurrection required a trained and faithful eye and an open heart, there was no way it could be a media event. Our vision has not only been distorted by the way the media packages events into manageable and titillating mouthfuls but has also been impoverished by a prevailing "scientism" that tries to flatten out reality by explaining everything away. I would not want to disparage the value of the many books on the Resurrection appearances (both scholarly and devotional). Historical and scientific research into the origins of Christianity are very important, because they can only enrich our understanding of the tradition. There is, however, no way we can *prove* that Jesus rose from the dead. Even if we could, what difference would it make? People believe many things. Belief for many people today means only a vague awareness of something. We are aware that millions of our fellow human beings are starving or undernourished. We believe that the proliferation of nuclear arms increases the likelihood of their use. We are aware of the social ills that eat away at the body politic. Beliefs like those are two a penny.

Just as many people in the first century did not experience the Resurrection because they did not know how, so today we are blind to its healing power because we are conditioned to resist it. We do not know how to experience the genuinely new. We long for news but do not want to open ourselves up to the invasion of the radically "new." The Church claims that the "event" of the Resurrection has no parallel. The Resurrection of Christ is unique and unrepeatable and, therefore, frustratingly unverifiable. There are no precedents, and the claims made for it in the New

Testament are wildly cosmic. The Resurrection is nothing less than the revelation of the reordering of all things. It turns everything upside down.

The New Testament presents us with three ways in which the risen Christ appears to his disciples. First are the "straightforward" Resurrection appearances. Jesus even invites his disciples to have breakfast on the beach (John 21). Yet even in this flesh and blood appearance, the disciples did not know that it was Jesus. Only later did it dawn on them who it was. "Yet no one dared ask him, 'Who are you?'" Even with this most obvious kind of Resurrection appearance, it takes time to recognize Jesus. Our eyes have to get used to it.

The second kind of appearance is more difficult to describe, because it is unlike experiencing someone physically present. The presence is real but out of the ordinary. For example, Jesus walks with two disciples on their way to Emmaus (Luke 24:13ff). They, like the disciples on the beach, do not at first know who he is, but when he breaks bread with them, their eyes are opened. It is not accidental that the context for our recognizing Jesus is often that of eating and drinking. The Church breaking bread, as it does day by day and week by week, is a privileged place of experiencing his presence.

St. Paul had a shattering experience of the risen Christ when he was on his way to Damascus (Acts 9). He had a blinding head-on collision, and his life was irrevocably changed. He had to wait to recover his sight and had to spend months in meditation to come to recognize what the experience meant for him. This kind of experience of the risen Christ is plainly different from the first. What unites them is the issue of sight, which is the issue of faith. "The way to faith," writes Abraham Heschel, "leads through acts of wonder and radical amazement. Awe precedes faith; it is the root of faith. We must grow in awe in order to reach faith. We must be guided by awe to be worthy of faith."[1] As we have seen, we are seriously impoverished in our longings, and because of this our capacity for awe and wonder is impaired. We live in a time when faith is thin, because our aching for what is above and beyond us has been anaesthetized and our capacity for wonder reduced to clever tricks.

The third way in which we encounter the living Christ is expressed in the crazed, bizarre poetic vision of the Apocalypse of St. John. Jesus is the "Lamb slain from the foundation of the world" (Rev. 5:6). This is not exactly an "appearance" but rather an explosive interpretation of who Jesus really was.

Two things confront us in the record of the Resurrection and of the way the early Christians understood it. One the one hand, it really was Jesus who appeared to his disciples. It wasn't a phantom or a hallucination. On the other hand, there is the strange fact that it took time for all of them to recognize him. They didn't know him because they didn't dare trust their experience. They, like us, lived under the tyranny of what we imagine *must* be the case. "Surely it can't be Jesus!" We all live under the spell of what we think our experience ought to be. None of us wants an experience that would turn things upside down. We experience the pain and joy of the Resurrection as an inner revolution of self-understanding. The technical term for that is *conversion*.

After breakfast, Jesus asked Peter three times (to Peter's great distress), "Do you love me?" This was the test of the Resurrection. Jesus then foretold Peter's own death and completed his discourse with two words, "Follow me!" The message of the Resurrection was clear for Peter's self-understanding: "Do you love me? You will die for it! Follow me!" This was the impact of the risen Christ on Peter. This was the impact of the risen Christ on Paul. The Resurrection was an event like no other. In it and through it all things were changed. How far are we prepared to entertain such an idea? We already think we know what is knowable. We are not open to surprises. How could we receive news of something that is (because of our fixed intellectual habits) inconceivable? "We must learn to overcome the sleek certainty and learn to understand that the existence of the universe is contrary to all reasonable expectations."[2] Learning to overcome our present certainties prepares us for the hurricane of the new, which is the Resurrection. "The world is not just there. It shocks us into amazement."[3]

Are we open to the shock of those ancient pictures of the Crucifixion that try to express the shattering and cosmic character of the dying and rising of Jesus? The author of the Epistle to the Colossians writes, "You have died, and your life is hid with Christ in God" (Col. 3:3, RSV). The "you" you worry about, the "you" you want to be in control, the "you" that is anxious and made frantic by conflicting desires—that manufactured "you" is dead! Thus the question shifts from, Did it really happen? to, What does it mean? and shifts yet again to, What does it mean for *me*? The mighty events of the Great Three Days of Good Friday, Holy Saturday, and Easter Day are for nothing less than the re-creation of the world. *That's what really happened!* You and I "happen" in a new way. The Resurrection is a homecoming!

St. John Chrysostom expressed it this way in one of his Easter sermons.

> *The first and last receive their reward. The rich and the poor rejoice together. Abstinent and heedless honor the day. Those who have fasted and those who have not fasted rejoice together. Let no one bewail his poverty, for the riches of all have appeared. Let none sorrow for sins, for forgiveness shines forth from the grave. Let none fear death—for the death of the Savior has redeemed us. He who embraced death has stamped it out. He who went down to Hell made Hell captive… Christ is risen and life lives!*

A strange thing has happened to my believing as I get older. I find that I believe in the Resurrection of Jesus Christ in a more concrete way, more literally, than I did twenty years ago. Yet I also find myself caught in—no, *enjoying* is a better word—a paradox. The point of the Resurrection is not found in our taking it literally, even though I believe it to be a fact. The Resurrection is not about dead carpenters being resuscitated and making it on to the ten o'clock news. The Resurrection of Jesus Christ isn't news in that sense. It is the explosion of the radically *New*. The Good News is about the New breaking in on our tired, frustrated, and divided world and filling us with awe, wonder, and longing. The theme of our pilgrimage has been summarized in the words, "God has fallen in love with you and wants you to come home." It is a homecoming that has been punctuated by tragedy. But if the cross is God's great tree, joining heaven and earth, then all that is tragic in life has a context and a possible meaning. There really is a homecoming. From the Christian point of view, tragedy is an important part of the story, but it is only a part. Tragedy is only a scene in a larger passion drama. Dante called that larger drama a *commedia*. Our sinning and our foolishness, our hurting and our suffering are all part of the Comedy of the Christian life, but they do not have the last word. The words of the creed, "He descended into hell," affirm that "there is no corner of God's universe over which his love has not brooded" (F. D. Maurice).

To accept that life is a "comedy" involves a willingness to enter into the drama fully and take the consequences. Abelard recognized God in his own sufferings and realized that he was in the presence of One who demanded unconditional service. We imagine we can negotiate with God. We might as well try to negotiate with a volcano or an earthquake. Are we willing to be shaped and transformed by a power outside our control? Do we want to live? This is the question posed by the Resurrection of Christ. The question, honestly faced, uncovers our neurotic fear of life. We dread the thought that something or someone should so seize hold of the mind the we "might be carried away and delivered over irrevocably to an unknown and unpredictable fate. At bottom, it is the ego's yearning dread of the Self."[4] This is a psychological way of talking about our longing for God and our dread of surrender.

The Resurrection is about our "yearning dread" of the "end" of our journey. All along we have had a companion on our pilgrimage who has been goading us with the Resurrection. Our uneasiness has to do with our committing the sin of refusing to be fully alive. To be fully alive is not to be in total control of our destiny. To be fully alive is to grow up into someone we are not yet. To be fully alive means our realizing that the Resurrection is *now*. It means giving up the comfort of what Marie-Louise von Franz calls "the Not-Yet." As long as I can go on convincing myself that this is not the time, that this is not the place, that I haven't yet arrived, I can always slip out of a difficult situation and make my pilgrimage an excuse for moving on. I do not want any form of closure or finality, because I would prefer "the phantasy that sometime in the future the real thing will come about."[5]

Franz Kafka called this continually aborting of new life on oneself "hesitation before birth." He wrote in his diary for January 1922, "Hesitation before birth. If there is transmigration of souls then I am not on the bottom rung. My life is hesitation before birth." Later he wrote, "Still unborn and already compelled to walk around the streets and speak to people." The Resurrection is not, in the first instance, a puzzling doctrine over which to make an intellectual decision. It is an invitation to life and to live *now*. Our journey has, in part, been to teach how much we dread and long for this new life.

What John Cheever claimed about the proper function of writing can be said of the purpose of the believing community. "The proper function of writing, if possible, is to enlarge people, to give them their risk, if possible to give them their divinity, not to cut them down."[6] This is precisely the inner work of the Resurrection. It is the power of God giving us our risk, enlarging our hearts, and, thereby, breathing new life into us. That is why I rely on the Spirit's marvelous working in novelists, poets, and other artists. John Cheever came to realize that his calling was to be an agent of the Spirit. "I think one has the choice with imagery, either to enlarge or diminish. At this point I find diminishment deplorable. When I was younger I thought it brilliant."[7] The imagery of the Christian Drama has been for our enlargement. It speaks to our longings and stretches our capacity for awe. It sows the seed of faith.

Easter brings together images of our woundedness and our longing for peace, for home, for glory. When Jesus appeared to his disciples (in John 20:19–31) he said, "Peace be with you!" and then showed them his hands and his side. There is no peace without wounds, no peace without responsibility, no peace without the risk of being sent off to God knows where. There is no peace without the goad and irritant of the Spirit. There is no private peace while others suffer, no peace without forgiveness and judgment.

An ancient legend recounts how the Devil tried to get into heaven by pretending to be the risen Christ. The Devil, being a master of disguises, took with him a contingent of demons made up as angels of light and shouted up at the gates of heaven, "Lift up your heads, O ye gates; and be ye lift up, ye everlasting doors; and the King of glory shall come in." The angels looked down on what they thought was their king returning in triumph from the dead. So they shouted back with joy and refrain from the psalm, "Who is the King of glory?" Then the devil made a fatal mistake. In every particular save one he was just like Christ. When the angels in heaven thundered, "Who is the King of glory?" the devil opened his arms and said, "I am!" In that act of arrogance he showed the angels his outstretched palms. There were no wounding marks of the nails. The angels of heaven refused to let the imposter in.

There is both pain and peace in the fellowship of pilgrims who have followed Christ to his Passion. We share in that Passion and peace whenever we break bread together and share the cup. We share in that Passion and peace whenever we give up our conceptual control of what *must* be the case, and open ourselves up to longing, awe, and wonder.

The risen Christ shows his disciples his hands and his side and in that simple act shows them God's and their mission in the world. It is to bring life to the world through the mystery of self-giving. Jesus says to us as surely as he said to his first disciples, "As the Father sent me even so send I you…" Our mission in the world is to be fully alive in such a way that others are enlivened by those who follow Christ. This is why God in Christ not only gave the disciples a great mission in the world, he also gave them the power to fulfill it. And "then he breathed on them, saying: Receive the Holy Spirit!"

Doubting Thomas suffered from the disease of the soul that we have identified as "hesitation before birth." Like him, we withdrawal from the peculiar pain of the challenge to live life to the full. Perhaps we fear life more than death? Who would not hesitate if living life to the full meant putting our hands into life's wounds? Is the Resurrection, in some sense, harder for us than the Crucifixion? At least our little crucifixions are familiar to us. We know what to expect from them. If we are at all sensitive we can see the torn face of humanity. But I wonder what in me needs to be touched? What do I fear most? Crucifixion or resurrection? Am I up to bearing the glory of a new life? The resurrection means trouble for us who are comfortable with being only half alive. What, then, in me needs to be raised from the dead? What part of you—long since rejected and forgotten—needs to be touched and restored to life?

The early Christians saw Christ as the Lord of history who suffered in the lives of their forebears as he suffered in them now. Melito of Sardis put it this way:

> *He was slain in Abel, shackled in Isaac, a pilgrim in Jacob, sold into slavery in Joseph, exposed to die in Moses, slaughtered in the sacrificial lamb, and presented in David, and stripped of honor in the prophets. He took flesh of the virgin, hung from the Cross, ascended the heights of Heaven, and when he rose from the dead he raised humankind from its tomb.*

Imagine what the living Christ is suffering, enduring *now* in us. Imagine what glory and peace he is bringing to us *now*. When we ask, Did it really happen? we must also ask, Am I really happening? Am I open to happening in new ways? The Resurrection happened and goes on happening so that you and I can really happen.

The young Mozart was driven to ask the same question of everyone he met: "Do you love me?" It is a question we silently ask all the time. I see it in the eyes of friends and strangers alike. Do you love me? It is a question about resurrection and new life. Our eyes soon glaze over so that the question is hidden once more. Do you love me? This is the question of the Resurrection. Our daring to ask it springs from our longing. Our repressing the question wells up from our terror. It is the question of our yearning dread. The Resurrection becomes a matter of choosing each other, of choosing life over death. When the answer to the question, Do you love me? is No!—when we treat each other as merely givers or deniers of approval—we have sided with death. The Resurrection is bound to get us into trouble.

"'Peace be unto you!' And he showed them his hands and his side." It is as if God in Christ is saying to us, "Hesitate no longer! Receive the Covenant of Reconciliation. Receive the wounding of my Peace! Receive the Resurrection! Receive *yourself*, ALIVE!" Easter is now!

STUDY QUESTIONS

1. Jones comments on the fantastic quality of the Resurrection, an event "resistant to cameras and tape recorders." "There is …no way we can *prove* that Jesus rose from the dead" (p. 151). What do you believe about this "revelation of the reordering of all things?" What aids your acceptance of this truth? What stands in the way?

2. Jones names two things that confront us in the record of the Resurrection and of the way the early Christians understood it: "On the one hand, it really was Jesus who appeared to his disciples.…On the other hand… it took time for all of them to recognize him" (p. 151). He suggests that recognizing Jesus goes against what we imagine must be the case; it demands conversion. How far are you prepared to entertain such an idea? Is there any experience in your life which prepares you to understand "that the existence of the universe is contrary to all reasonable expectations"? (p. 151).

3. "The Good News," Jones writes, "is about the New breaking in on our tired, frustrated, and divided world and filling us with awe, wonder, and longing" (p. 152–153). The One who breaks in demands unconditional service. "Are we willing to be shaped and transformed by a power outside our control?" In what areas of your life have you experienced the "dread of surrender"? What longings keep you near taking the risk?

4. Jones asserts, "The Resurrection is not, in the first instance, a puzzling doctrine over which to make an intellectual decision. It is an invitation to live and to live *now*" (p. 154). How does this definition of the Resurrection compare with traditional doctrine? What comes to your mind as you recite the Nicene Creed and state, "On the third day he rose again, in accordance with the Scriptures"? Which image enlarges you, gives you your risk? Are the two images so very different?

5. "What, then, in [you] needs to be raised from the dead? What part of you—long since rejected and forgotten—needs to be touched and restored to life?" (p.156).

13.
EASTER—THE HOPE OF GLORY

Do you love me? is the unspoken question shining in everyone's eyes. The Resurrection is not only God's answer to our question, it also reflects the question back to us. That is why we fear it even as we long for it. Easter Day is the day of glory and terror. It is sometimes called "the Eighth Day of Creation." It took seven days to make the world, and Easter Day is the eighth day, a day of the new creation. The Resurrection, therefore, is the action of a God who comes to us as a challenge to embrace the new rather than as a comforting idea to bolster up preexisting prejudices. This God is a wild and healing presence rather than a dry philosophical notion. This God stirs up in us a yearning to serve in response to his great love for us.

On Easter Day the Passion Play that has been working itself out in us comes to a conclusion (although it would be a mistake to think of it as an ending. It is a conclusion with a future!). The play runs in our blood whether we believe or not. If we are honest, we know the drama well. D. H. Lawrence wrote of it like this:

And if, in the changing phases of a man's life
I fall in sickness and in misery
my wrists seem broken and my heart seems dead
and strength is gone, and my life
is only the leavings of a life:

and still, among it all, snatches of lovely
oblivion, and snatches of renewal
odd, wintry flowers upon the withered stem,
yet new, strange flowers
such as my life has not brought forth before,
new blossoms of me—

then I must know that still I am in the hands
of the unknown God,
he is breaking me down to his oblivion
to send me forth on a new morning, a new man.[1]

The drama goes on, recognized or not, in every human heart. I long for and dread the possibility of "new blossoms of me" no matter how cold and wintry the weather in my soul. I want to give up my love affair with death. Easter is the day on which that love affair is shown up for what it really is. We live in a world in love with death, in love with things that pass away. Our misplaced passion for security is killing us. Think of the arsenals of death assembled all around the world in the name of global security. From our most intimate relations to international alliances, we wall up our hearts against the invasion of the Resurrection.

What does the word *God* mean to us? *God* is a sign that only a strong love can heal us. If the word *God* doesn't mean that, then it doesn't mean anything. Resurrection believing brings us into contact with the God who knows and loves us.

The Resurrection introduces an uncomfortable newness into our relationships and social arrangements. It even affects our political views. It speaks to the tension between our longing for and our fear of each other. It means giving up the security blankets of our tired skepticism and lazy sentimentality. In our society, there is a great deal of what I can only describe as a sort of cruising unbelief. People nowadays don't want anyone to question their *un*belief. It used to be the other way around, but many today have never had much of a belief from which to fall away. Extreme skepticism is as irrational as unexamined sentimentality. Both prevent us from acknowledging our wildest longings. The former tells us that our longings are childish and adolescent. The latter domesticates them and makes them safe.

At first sight our skepticism seems justified. The news is often about money-grubbing evangelists or venal politicians. Two graffiti in the New York City subway system sum up our skepticism: "God is alive. He just doesn't want to get involved"; and (referring to the Vietnam War) "We are the unwilling, led by the unqualified, doing the unnecessary, for the ungrateful." I have, however, come to believe that skepticism is a greater lie than sentimentality. When someone tells me that he's only being realistic, it is usually a prelude to his doing something shabby. When someone calls himself a realist, it often means he is preparing to do something of which he is secretly ashamed. I wonder if our skepticism is a cloak for our shame? The Resurrection promises to rid us of both. Our skepticism protects us against the possibility and the risk of new life. The truth is that we don't want God to break through. We like to see the failure of the best so that we can have the satisfaction of being able to say, "See, I told you so!" Yet we ache for communion with one another, even as we dread it. The Resurrection means losing our fixed place in a fixed world by recovering the longings that we thought we had to give up when we became "adults." The trouble is that we still do not know that for which we long. We do not know our heart's desire. We take our cue of how we are supposed to feel and act from others. Walker Percy's hero (a psychiatrist) in *The Thanatos Syndrome* confessed that he was amazed by the number of his patients who were at a loss or felt crazy because they did not know what to do with themselves. They were crazed or unhappy because they didn't know how to "do things right."

> *I don't mean right in the moral sense, but right in the way people on TV or in books or in movies always do things right. Even when such actor-people go wrong, go nuts, they do it in a proper rounded off way, like Jane Fonda having a breakdown on TV. "I can't even have a successful nervous breakdown!" cried Ella, wringing her hands. She thought she had to go nuts in a poetic way, like Ophelia singing sad songs and jumping in the creek with flowers in her hair. How do I know what to do, Doctor? Why can't you tell me? What I want to tell them is, this is not the Age of Enlightenment but the Age of Not Knowing What To Do.* [2]

It is hard for us to surrender to our wildest longings, to open ourselves up to glory, when we don't know what to think or do. If we do not understand ourselves to be part of a great love story, our passion drives us crazy, our hopes turn sour, and our longings become a torment. If, however, we pay attention to our longings, we would find that their real aim, in the Story, is glory. That is what we are about: glory. Glory is the name we give to a life passionately lived in all its fullness. We are destined for glory. This is what we were made for.

The question is, How should we celebrate the glory promised in the Resurrection? When we see the question, Do you love me? in another's eye, we see the longing for glory. We add to their glory when we are able to find a way of saying yes to others. The Resurrection disturbs me a great deal, because it sends me off on pilgrimage in search for glory. In its light I can see only too clearly my own homelessness, my fear of newness and the strange presences of other people. The more I enter the mystery of the Resurrection, the more I enter into the vulnerability of God, the more I find myself to be (as we have seen) "an experiment in vulnerability." God's glory is in God's willingness to be wounded for the sake of love.

The Resurrection, then, is like falling into a hole. Alice fell down the rabbit hole. She dropped into a totally new world. The risen Christ presents me with a new world, and its newness and strangeness are present in every human being I meet. I am sometimes caught up in the fantasy that everyone is on the lookout for God, searching for glory. I catch people on buses, at airports, at work, at dinner—they "go off" somewhere for a few moments and are in another world. They are on pilgrimage, looking for God or for someone or something that will make them happy. People are beautifully vulnerable at those moments. They are bearers of mystery—enigmas to me and to themselves. Then the moment passes, and we are back inside our old wary selves.

Living the Resurrection means being willing to fall into the great chasm we call love. We are familiar with the phrase *falling in love*. We are to fall into God and are on pilgrimage to discover a new way of imagining ourselves and our world. I am nervous about the phrase *falling in love* because I am afraid that it will reveal to you the fact that I am unwilling to grow up. I feel naked and embarrassed when I talk about desire. C. S. Lewis wrote:

> *In speaking of this desire... I feel a certain shyness. I am almost committing an indecency. I am trying to rip open the inconsolable secret in each one of you—the secret which hurts so much that you take revenge on it by calling it names like nostalgia and romanticism and adolescence, the secret also which pierces with such sweetness that, when, in very intimate conversation, the mention of it becomes imminent, we grow awkward and affect to laugh at ourselves; the secret we cannot hide and cannot tell.*

We cannot tell because we have no words to describe the desire that is never quite fulfilled. We cannot hide the desire, because it is continually revealing itself in our attempts to be open about it or to hide it. Lewis confesses that he is trying to weave a spell but reminds his readers that "spells are used for breaking enchantments as well as inducing them." We need a spell to break the terrible enchantment of death in our culture. The Resurrection breaks the spell by making us nomads of the Spirit. Our blood is Bedouin. Love, writes Laurens Van der Post, "is the aboriginal tracker on the faded desert of [my] lost self; and so I came to live my life not by conscious plan or prearranged design but as someone following the flight of a bird." That is the way life is to be lived by pilgrims of the Resurrection. We are children of the Eighth Day, but we don't know it. We don't know our own story! We are "between stories." Our narrowly nationalistic stories (always in conflict with one another) will bring the world to ruin if we are not willing to be open to a story that will bind the human race together. The witness of religion at its best and highest is that God is One. Because God is One, humanity is one also. God is everyone's pedigree. God is either the Father and Mother of everyone or of no one. God's image is imprinted in us all or in none.

We have, as yet, no common story, and the stories we *do* have are not functioning too well. In Jesus Christ, the story is written in a language easily understood by everyone. We can read the outline of the story in the eyes of everyone we meet. We already know the way the story begins with the question, Do you love me? Augustine puts these words into the mouth of God, "I am in all languages—Greek, Latin, Hebrew. The tongues of all nations are mine, because I am one with all people."

There are people of other religions learning the great Love Story in their own way. I do not presume to judge them. Many of them have helped me and continue to help me walk the Pilgrim's Way. For me, however, the Way is Christ but not the Christ who is manipulable, the pawn of religious imperialists. The Christ I seek to follow is often hidden from me, with me, yet ahead of me, stretching my loving to include more and more of the Creation. I believe every one shares, to some extent, in the life of this Christ, since the mission is to form us all into One People.

I love the story of the disciples going fishing. Navigation is a good metaphor of the new life in Christ. Sailing is good for the soul, and the early Christians were called "wanderers for the love of God." That is what we are called to be—wanderers for the love of God, calling our brothers and sisters into an ever-deepening and widening fellowship.

What does the Resurrection signify? As we have seen, it points to an irrepressible capacity in each one of us to go beyond ourselves and re-vision the world. The unacknowledged echoes of the Resurrection are all around us. Artists, in particular, are the bearers of the signs of Resurrection. Ansel Adams, the photographer, wrote in his memoirs, "The relatively few authentic creators of our time possess a resonance with eternity. The resonance, I think, is worth fighting for, and it takes tremendous energy and sacrifice." The energy working within us is the Resurrection.

The Resurrection story begins with the question, Do you love me? and leads to a second: Where is home? The answers we see and hear in the life, death, Resurrection of Christ. God in Christ says, "I love you. Where love is, I am. Where I am is home." God has fallen in love with you and wants you to come home. The homecoming is for everyone. The best way I know to express the universality of this good news of glory is to understand that the world is a wedding to which everyone is invited. The author of the Apocalypse spoke of "the marriage supper of the Lamb." Imagine all of us, the whole human family, seated together around one big table, breaking bread together, enjoying a great feast. We are called to be both hosts and guests to one another and understand that we are bound together in our eating and drinking. All our eating and drinking has something of the sacramental about it. Every meal is capable of bringing us all closer together. Think of Plato's *Symposium*—the occasion when friends gathered round a table to tell "wonderful stories of the meaning of their longing." Think of Dante's *Convivio*—another banqueting table around which we are to sit, eat, make merry, and talk about great things. Reality is convivial. Our glory is to be found in a symposium. A wedding banquet is a wonderful and restorative metaphor. The table is so large that everyone has a place. No one is left out. There is enough to eat.

The theme of a great banquet at the end of time has its roots in what is called "the Bedouin consciousness" of desert people, out of which sprang the biblical literature. The desert dwellers knew that the "outside" world was dangerous, and there were, therefore, strict rules of hospitality in the face of common dangers. It was and is a great crime to betray someone with whom you have just broken bread. Rules of hospitality were strictly adhered to. In the Old Testament, Abraham is to be the host of a great throng of people who will come from the East and the West to gather at the banquet at the end of time.

We could go through the New Testament picking out images that reinforce the picture of feasting and celebration. The parable of the Prodigal Son brings together the themes of forgiveness and feasting. A wandering son, thought to be lost and dead, is brought home to great rejoicing. Think of the parable of the Good Samaritan. A man—wounded and broken—is given hospitality by one who is himself an outcast. When the early Christians read Psalm 23— "Thou preparest a table before me"—they thought of the great table at the end of time that would be a place of fellowship and safety and welcome where everyone would have enough. Eating and drinking together are central to our understanding of and living the Resurrection. It is no accident that we find accounts of the feeding miracles in all four Gospels. Jesus is the nurturer. Jesus is the one who gives himself to us as food. Jesus is also a scandal, because he will eat with *anybody*. He will eat with the rejected and the outcast. Jesus, the one who makes room for all people, has no place himself. "The birds of the air have their nests. The foxes have holes, but the Son of man has nowhere to lay his head."

Hospitality is a sign of the Resurrection, a sign of new life, a sign of the reordering of the universe around one great table. We know from experience that, when patterns of hospitality break down, human beings suffer terrible cruelties. Is it possible for us to imagine a community where *everyone* is welcome and where there is enough? If hospitality is a sign of Resurrection, its denial is the harbinger of death. There is perverse joy we sometimes experience in excluding others from our particular table. Our longing for acceptance and approval is often accompanied by a desire to exclude others. To be part of an "in" group requires that there be a large number (the larger the better) of outsiders. There is something very satisfying about exclusiveness.

The indiscriminate welcoming of all people to the Supper of the Lamb is very threatening. The notion that *everybody* is welcome radically reorders our world. The question we posed earlier remains. Do we fear resurrection more than crucifixion? We choose death when we refuse to come to the banquet out of snobbery or fear. The Resurrection calls us *all* to life, to the possibility of new personal attachments and to new communal responsibilities. No wonder we resist it. The Love of God is indiscriminate and out of control. No wonder many of us try to organize another banquet somewhere else. There are many such banquets—focused on religion, ideology, or prejudice. Not everyone is invited to these parties. The guest list is carefully vetted, and there is a clear line drawn between those who are "in" and those who are "out."

Not long ago I was asked to give the invocation at the annual luncheon of the Associated Press. Invocations at luncheons are a strange genre in a country that sets great store by the separation of church and state. An invocation is a short sermon under the guise of an uplifting prayer to an all-purpose god. The main speaker on this occasion was former president Richard Nixon. He talked about American foreign policy. In the middle of his address he said, "Anticommunisim is not a *policy* of the United States: it is a *faith*." It is not difficult to imagine other world leaders (of Libya and the Soviet Union, for example) saying something like, "Anti-Americanism is not a policy; it is a faith." It is very difficult to get people of warring faiths to sit at a meal together around one table. It is hard for people who are in love with death to turn to the reality of the resurrection. We live in a world of warring ideologies. Those ideologies are the prisms through which we see reality.

We need something around which to gather. Ideology won't bind us together; neither will an exclusivist "faith." We need a *symposium*, a *convivio*. We need a table. Resurrection believing means sitting at *one* table to which everyone is invited. Seeing that we have one destiny and destination is part of the glory of being human. Glory is being willing to enjoy the stretching allegiance demanded of this table fellowship. The believer is willing to begin to draw out the poison arrows we fire at one another in the course of our social contracts. We wound each other with the arrows of indifference and malice. Hurts (deliberate and unmeant) pierce the hearts of our brothers and sisters. Some are left to die, like St. Sebastian, full of arrows. We need a healing space where such arrows can be pulled out. Around the table of the Resurrection we help pull out the arrows from those around us. Our table fellowship requires us to do this, because the Resurrection always brings challenge, healing, and forgiveness. The questions at the Wedding Banquet are, Who do I need to forgive? Who needs to forgive me? The Resurrection is expressed in small ways—in the writing of a letter, the making of a phone call, even the tilt of the head in loving, if silent, recognition. The Resurrection is a breakthrough in hospitality that sees the world is a wedding to which everyone is invited.

Why do we continue to resist what we seek? Why are we terrified of glory, of being in all its fullness? Walker Percy's psychiatrist says, "I seldom give people drugs. If you do, they may feel better for a while, but they'll never find out what the terror is trying to tell them." What is our terror trying to tell us? The world is a wedding and everyone is invited.

STUDY QUESTIONS

1. "Do you love me?" is the question that is raised again and again as we play on the fringes of belief in the Resurrection. Is this a question that can ever be answered to our satisfaction? What tensions does it reveal between our longing for and our fear of each other? How does the Resurrection speak to these tensions?

2. Take a pause and hold silently for yourself moments when you have lived life passionately in all its fullness and moments when you have failed to do so. What were they like?

3. After quoting C. S. Lewis, Jones talks of the secret we cannot tell—"We cannot tell because we have no words to describe the desire that is never quite fulfilled" (p. 163). In a world of words, this can feel like quite a disability. How do you react to the absence of adequate verbiage? What other ways of communicating are at your disposal?

4. Jones states that "the indiscriminate welcoming of all people to the Supper of the Lamb is very threatening. The notion that *everybody* is welcome radically reorders our world." Then he asks, "Do we fear resurrection more than crucifixion?" (p. 166). How do you respond? "Why are we terrified of glory, of being in all its fullness? …What is our terror trying to tell us?" (pp. 167–68).

14.
THE DRAMA IN OUR BONES

Our passion for pilgrimage brings us home to God, to each other, and to ourselves. It may seem ironic that we have gone on this pilgrimage through the desert of our longings only to find that we end up where we began. God's great gift to me is to enjoy me so much that I can be at home with myself. Reluctantly I am able to admit that I really do belong to God, that the love affair is true. The drama of God's love for me is in my bones. The promise of glory is in my blood.

One of my favorite feasts of the Church is the celebration of the Assumption of the Blessed Virgin Mary. We do this every year on August 15. Parts of the Church do it with a great deal of enthusiasm. Other parts are either nervous or severely critical of the celebration. The Church has never known how to treat Mary. She is either adored (often inappropriately) or ignored altogether. The Assumption is, however, a feast worth examining because it can tell us something about ourselves, about our pilgrimage and our destiny. It speaks to me of the ongoing drama in my bones. Called the *Dormition* or the Falling Asleep of Our Lady by the Orthodox Church, the feast celebrates the destiny and place of Mary who is the Holy *Theotokos*, or God-bearer, for the salvation of the world.

Traditionally, Mary, the Mother of God, is the key figure, after Jesus, in the Christian understanding of redemption. She has a vital role in the Passion Play. Perhaps that is why there is as much controversy over the person of Mary as there is over her Son. Many Protestants think of her as a distinguished but dead Roman Catholic! When I was growing up in England, I attended a church dedicated to her, but I do not remember her name ever being mentioned. Some Christian feminists reject her as a model for women today because of her traditional passivity and submissiveness. Mary is seen as a mere projection of the male desire for an ever-available mother. Other feminists try to turn her into an almost Amazonlike figure whose virginity was so "fertile" that it could produce a son without any help from a mere male. Insofar as she has been used as a means to reinforce the subjugation of women or to allow men to sentimentalize women by putting them on a pedestal, devotion to Mary is to be deplored. There have been excesses, but the abuses do not justify our ignoring her. Mary must have been quite a woman, and it would be strange for Christians to take no notice of her. She is, in fact, a model of Christian pilgrim, male as well as female. The Passion Story was lived out in her in a special way.

There are, however, other difficulties that surround this particular feast, similar to ones that people have with the Resurrection. The question, Did it really happen? is asked of the Assumption of Mary. The dogma states that Mary was bodily assumed into heaven. That is quite a mouthful to swallow. The skeptic in me murmurs, "Believe *that* if you like!" Words like *heaven* and *bodily* present apparent insurmountable difficulties for those of us who look at life with a literalist squint. If we are devoid of poetic imagination, we think that the dogma states that Mary rose like a rocket to a place somewhere beyond the solar system. But heaven, for a start, isn't a place like any other place. You don't "go" there in the same way that you go to New York or Los Angeles. The word *bodily*, however, presumes not only that there's a place to go but that there is a "someone" who is going. Our commitment to literalism gets in the way of meaning. The dogma means that who Mary was in her fullness of person (in all her glory), recognizable and particular, is with God forever. That is what the feast celebrates. A monk (when asked about the Assumption of the Blessed Virgin Mary) shocked a television audience in England some years ago by testily answering, "If she isn't in heaven, then where the hell is she?" The problem is that the Church has made matters worse by promulgating dogmas as if they were scientific facts. We find the same confusion around the dogma of the Virgin Birth. Mary's "virginity" is not so much about her physical condition as about the risk and vulnerability of God in God's willingness to dwell among us. As with the Resurrection, so with the Virgin Birth: as I get older I have come to believe in these doctrines more and more literally. At the same time I also believe that their "literalism" is not the main point.

The Church hasn't helped matters by not having a very good record with regard to its attitude to sexuality. The insistence on virginity, the rule in some parts of the Church of a celibate, all-male clergy seems to reinforce the downgrading of sexuality and the body. The Church even went so far as to affirm the perpetual virginity of Mary. One of my teachers, a great Orthodox theologian, was asked why the Church insisted on the perpetual virginity of Mary. He replied, "Is it conceivable to the Mary, the Holy God-Bearer, once having given birth to the Christ, would then take up a bourgeois relationship with Joseph?" It is an amusing answer but not really an adequate one. It is difficult to justify the doctrine except to say that the word *virginity* became synonymous with total dedication and faithfulness. Jesus, himself, was sometimes referred to as the Arch-Virgin because of his wonderful self-giving on the cross.

The problem is with our approach to dogma. Dogma is supposed to lead us into the Drama of God's love for us. Instead, it is made into a stumbling block. A dogma is the first word on a subject that serves as a platform to catapult us into mystery, not the last word of a definition that tries to circumscribe it. Dogma suffers from the same kind of nonsense to which the Bible is often subjected. Imagine this as a word from Scripture:

This is what the Lord says: There was once a goose that laid a golden egg each day. And the farmer's wife, who owned the goose, delighted in the riches that those eggs brought her. She was an avaricious woman, however, and could not wait patiently from day to day for her daily egg. She decided to kill the goose and get the eggs all at once.

An atheist... scoffed: You call that the word of God! A goose that lays golden eggs! It just goes to show the absurdity of your scriptures...

[T]he scholar... reacted thus: The Lord clearly tells us that there was a goose that laid golden eggs. If the Lord says

this, then it must be true, no matter how absurd it appears to our poor human minds. Now you will ask... how an egg, while not ceasing to be an egg, can, at the same time, be golden. Different schools of religious thought attempt to explain it differently. But what is called for here is an act of faith in this mystery that baffles human understanding.

There was even a preacher who, inspired by that text, traveled through towns and villages zealously urging people to accept the fact that God created golden eggs at some point in history.

Moral: "It is better to teach people the evils of avarice than promote belief in golden eggs."[1] So it is with the dogmas of the Church. It is better to enter into the drama of God's love than to wait on the edge until every dogma is properly understood. Dogmas are like the love letters that lovers keep and look at from time to time to remind them of the story that binds them together. Faith (which is prepared for, as we have seen, by our being open to wonder and awe) comes before understanding. Love doesn't work that way. We *fall* in love and then spend the rest of our lives trying to explain to ourselves what happened. Sometimes we love unwisely, but that too contributes to our struggle to understand. I would rather be able to love fully and freely than to be able to define it.

The Feast of the Assumption of the Blessed Virgin Mary is about love and how it lives and moves in us. It is about Mary, God, and us. Dogma is about us. Dogmas about Mary are dogmas about God's falling in love with us. I can remember being gently reprimanded by a fellow student in seminary when I questioned his having a statue of the Blessed Virgin Mary in his room. "Mary teaches me about the humility of God," he replied. When I see a picture of the Madonna and Child, I see a sign of a wonderful drama in which God makes himself weak, vulnerable, human, and available for my sake.

All Christian doctrine is, at bottom, not only about God but also about us. Dogmas always tell me something about myself. One of the reasons the early Church gave for the necessity of the

Incarnation was that we needed to have Jesus around simply to remind us what a human being really is. We forget. The occupational hazard of human beings is our forgetfulness, our built-in amnesia. We need all the help we can get. Our habitual memory loss with regard to who we are and what we are about has serious consequences. We hurt and are hurt in return when we forget. I need the bundle of love letters that we call the creeds. I need the reminders that I am an actor in a Passion Drama that is bringing me home. When I wonder who I am and where I am heading, I read one of these love letters, and it sets me on the Pilgrim's Way once more.

It used to be said that philosophy was the discipline of saying what everybody knew in terms that nobody could understand, while theology stated the impossible in terms of the incomprehensible. These are unfair statements, but one can see how they came about. What is it that will wake us up? What is it that might (just might) give our lives some moral bite so that we don't fade away into terminal boredom? The bundle of love letters needs to be read over and over again to keep us on course. Sometimes, when I read them over, my eyes cloud over with tears. I am reminded that it is possible to get lost. It is possible to sin—really sin. A sense of guilt overcomes me when I realize that I am sometimes a false lover. I am also assured of the promise of healing and forgiveness. I am reminded of the fact that I cannot only lose my way but that I have a Lover who is always searching for me. The bundle of love letters (the Scriptures, the creeds, the Stories of the Lovers of God, the saints) are not the love itself but tokens, signs, reminders of it.

Dogmas are about our identity, about who we are. Dogmas help us find ways to talk about our commitments and, if we don't know what they are, to find out. Sometimes they strike us as absurd or outdated, at other times, arbitrary and even cruel. What has been awful in the course of human history is the way people have used certain dogmas for their own ends. They have taken the bundle of love letters and quoted bits and pieces of them out of context in order to bully or embarrass others. Heresy is precisely the partial use of the love letters. The phrases that we like best become our unexamined assumptions that are used to hurt others. For example, the love letters bear witness in many places to the importance of order in human affairs. There is a "natural law" that allows love to run free. The "dogma" of natural law, however, was often applied to society in such a way that it frustrated and inhibited social change. The old hymn put it this way:

> *The rich man in his castle,*
> *The poor man at his gate—*
> *God made then high and lowly*
> *And ordered their estate.*

It takes a dramatic dogmatic upheaval to break through such sanctified self-interest. The love letters must be read as a whole if the Passion Play is to be understood aright. Dogmas are a stumbling block to belief for a great many people, because they do not know what they are. I spend much of my time trying to explain, not so much the dogmas themselves, as the kind of thing a dogma is. The great dogmas of the church, enshrined in the ancient creeds, are actually radical statements about us human beings and our relationships to God and to each other. They point to glory. They are not only the intimate communications between lovers, they are also the manifesto of revolution. They are marching orders.

The doctrine of the Holy and Undivided Trinity, for example, is about us. It continually challenges us with a vision of community, of unity in diversity that stretches us to new ways to develop a humane and humanizing society. The doctrine of the Incarnation, the doctrine that God is here among us, means that God is to be found and seen in the flesh of all our sisters and brothers. The love letters insist that every human being matters. Such dogmas are explosive.

What Franz Kafka wrote about books, we might say about dogma.

> *If the book we are reading does not wake us, as with a fist*
> *hammering on our skull, why then do we read it? So that it*

should make us happy? Good God, we would also be happy
if we had no books, and such books as make us happy we
could, if need be, write ourselves. But what we must have are
those books which come upon us like ill-fortune, and distress
us deeply, like the death of one we love better than ourselves,
like suicide. A book must be an ice-axe to break the sea
frozen inside us.[2]

If this is true of books, how much more true is it of the mighty
doctrines of the Christian faith, understood as love letters from a
God who called us into being because of his love for us. The love
letters teach us how to read each other. They teach us to see the
unspoken question, Do you love me? in the eyes of others. When
we try to read each other, when we try to understand what we are
about, the doctrines of the Church can come upon us like an ice
axe to break the sea frozen inside us. We need such an ice axe to
break the frozen depths of the soul. Dogma is a kind of spiritual
sledgehammer to break open the depths within us. Mary is one of
the ice axes of God that reveal to us God's humility and love.

"But let me tell you," says a character in Eliot's *The Cocktail*
Party,

that to approach the stranger
Is to invite the unexpected, release a new force,
Or let the genie out of the bottle.
It is to start a train of events
Beyond your control...

Isn't this exactly what Mary did? She invited the unexpected.
What a metaphor her pregnancy is! She becomes the container of
the uncontainable. She is the womb of God. And, as such she is a
model for both men and women (not just women) of the power of
the energy of God working within us. When I encounter God,
when I become pregnant with the divine, it is like meeting a
stranger. I am letting the genie out of the bottle. Who knows what
might happen? I am sent on pilgrimage.

What does Mary tell us about ourselves? The Assumption of Mary affirms the status of all human beings as made after the image of God. If we remember that the doctrine is about God and God's humility, graciousness, and availability, we will not get hooked into thinking that something is being pulled over on us and that we've been tricked into worshiping Mary. As one English Methodist friend of mine responded to his Protestant critics who questioned his devotion to Mary, "Why won't you let me love her?" Why won't you let yourself love her? In loving her we might learn to love ourselves and so love each other. Just as she is termed the Mother of God, so might each of us claim (after the ancient tradition that called St. James, the brother of Jesus, the Brother of God) that we are the sisters and brothers of God. This is what the love letters are trying to tell us. We can't do better than that!

Is it any wonder that the Church has wanted to honor Mary, the mother of Jesus? No wonder the tradition honors her joys and sorrows in the rosary and struggles to find words to pay her due homage. The love letters are full of references to her. Wisdom says, "Come, eat of my bread and drink of the wine I have mixed" (Prov. 9:1–6, RSV). Just as Wisdom invites us to share in the banquet of God, so Mary, who nourished her son at her breast, invites us to share in the same wedding feast. Yet, she is "the daughter of her son" (as Dante puts it in the *Paradiso*) and is thus nurtured by the one she nurtured. Such is the economy of love. We feed each other. We are even agents of the Resurrection to one another.

St. Brendan (in Frederick Buechner's version of his life) exiles himself to a barren island. He is half mad with guilt. He has lost his way and is a "shipwreck of a man." The pilgrimage has come to a standstill. Brendan is visited by St. Brigit who tells him to get moving. He fears to go where he is known because people only want to hear of his voyages, which, to him, amount to nothing. "Go to a place where nobody knows you then. Find a place where there's folk who've never heard of your voyaging and all that. Bring Christ to them, Brendan, and in God's good time perhaps they'll bring him again to you." Here is the mystery of exchange that I find in the love letters. I often find the very gift for which I long when, bereft of it myself, I try to give it to others. Brigit's visit to Brendan's remote island begins a healing process in Brendan. She knew that the gospel is for the shipwrecked. "Brigit called Brendan out of the grave that day as surely as ever Christ called Lazarus out of it. Perhaps it was the greatest wonder she ever worked."[3] What greater act of love is there than calling another from the grave? This is what God's action in Jesus Christ is all about.

Mary is important because she was willing to be the instrument of God. In her, we see that (as Tertullian, the second-century theologian, said) "the flesh is the hinge of salvation." Mary is important because Christianity is an earthy religion. It is based in flesh and blood and in bread and wine. It is grounded in the ordinary and the commonplace. Ironically, the Virgin Birth was insisted upon in the early years because there were those who said that Jesus wasn't really human. He was some heavenly being. Mary was the guarantee that Jesus was really one of us. This crude insistence on the material is emphasized in the Gospel: "Truly, truly, I say to you, unless you eat the flesh of the Son of man and drink his blood, you have no life in you; he who eats my flesh and drinks my blood has eternal life, and I will raise him up at the last day" (John 6:53–59, RSV). There are many ways of interpreting this, but what strikes home is the insistence on the material, on the here and now, on the necessity of throwing ourselves into life.

Think, for a moment, of Mary. She has just said Yes! to the baby, to the longed-for unknown. She contemplates the future stretching of her belly, and her own stretching by the child that will be born. It is a common experience for mothers. It is a metaphor that others in our culture need to appropriate—both men and women. Giving birth is an ordeal, and we, pregnant with God, are to give birth to a new understanding of ourselves. We are called to assist at our own birth. I know of no greater adventure. I know of no other way to describe it but as an ongoing drama of resurrection. The love letters never cease to amaze me.

George Emery, an old friend and expert on Christian mythology, sent us a Christmas poem not long ago about Mary as the sign and promise of new life breaking out in us.

To understand ordeals underground
Following the footsteps of the Lord
Into our own identity
Is difficult. As a new baby
Finds his mother to be another,
And she a new person,
Mary saw God in her son,
Beholds him still for us
Both there and on the cross.

This describes our inner pilgrimage. It is an underground ordeal into the mystery of who we are. Through the agency of others we become new persons. Anne Sexton contributed to the bundle of love letters when she wrote,

Oh, Mary
Gentle Mother,
open the door and let me in.
A bee has stung your belly with faith.
Let me float in it like a fish.
Let me in! Let me in!
I have been born many times, a false Messiah,
but let me be born again
into something true.[4]

Dogma is about us. Mary is about us. God's gift to us is the freedom to follow him into the depths of who we are. We follow the footsteps of our Lord into our own identity… to be born again and again and again. What freedom there is in my not having to be my own messiah! What freedom there is in meeting him in the sign of the Wedding Banquet, the Eucharist, the table that has room for everybody.

The Feast of the Assumption of the Blessed Virgin Mary is not without its difficulties, but it can serve as a much-needed ice axe to break open the sea frozen inside us. There are certainly other ways of understanding Mary and her role. But this, at least, we can say—

that the traditional title Mother of God (the Holy *Theotokos*) challenges us with questions about our own commitments or lack of them. Honoring her could be the first blow of the ice axe. It could be a way of not only acknowledging the drama in our bones but also of setting us on pilgrimage into the mystery of how we can be born again into something true.

Study Questions

1. Jones promises, "God's great gift to me is to enjoy me so much that I can be at home with myself" (p. 169). What kind of God would give this gift? Where do you struggle against truly receiving it?

2. Native American storytellers will sometimes begin a story by saying, "Now I'm not really sure if it happened this way, but I know it is true…" Jones echoes this tone in his discussion of the Assumption of Mary when he states, "Our commitment to literalism gets in the way of the meaning" (p. 170). What do you believe is the literal truth about Mary? What do you believe is the meaning? What dangers exist in separating these two approaches? What would we miss if we failed to seek both understandings?

3. Writing about the drama of God's love and how dogma enters into that drama, Jones writes, "Faith… comes before understanding… I would rather be able to love fully and freely than to be able to define it" (p. 172). How does this compare with your basic approach to life? How does it compare to the church? To society? Where else in our lives are we invited first to experience and only then to understand?

4. Jones writes, "Giving birth is an ordeal, and we, pregnant with God, are to give birth to a new understanding of ourselves. We are called to assist at our own birth" (p. 177). What are your experiences of birth? How are they like and unlike your experiences of resurrection? What other graphic images of co-creation might help to describe the mystery of throwing ourselves into life?

15.
THE FIRE OF LOVE

We began our pilgrimage with the assertion that the cycle of the Church's Year gives us an opportunity to deepen our wildest longings. We are now nearing the end of the journey. Its whole purpose has been so that "broken bones may joy." On our pilgrimage we have found "hatred of God" and even cursing God to be signs of our longing. The burning inside us, whether fueled by love or by hatred, goes on. A terrible fire raged, for example, in the heart of Malo, a monk in Frederick Buechner's *Brendan*. He hated God for the brutal killing of his wife and babies. At the end of the book Malo confesses to Brendan, "There's part of me that curses him still perhaps, though with most of me I've forgiven him."[1] What led Malo to forgive God was one particular experience on his pilgrimage. A crazed and dying monk mistook Malo for Christ.

> *I couldn't tell him I wasn't the one he thought I was but only Malo, bitter and hateful as ever. I even saw why I couldn't too. It was he touched my heart with his daftness and his dying. It was because I knew I'd be dying myself one day and that made us brothers… I'd taken him to my heart you see.*

At the end we are to take each other to our hearts. We are all sisters and brothers in death. We learn compassion by seeing the daftness and dying in others. Malo could do nothing about the crazed monk dying, no more than he could have saved his wife and children, many years earlier. But then, Christ could not keep himself from dying when the time came. "All at once I saw in myself the helplessness of Christ. That's when I forgave him." The pilgrim in the Way of Love has to learn to "forgive God" and, through that, to learn that there is a way of loving, holding the world together, that is radically new.

I sometimes drift in and out of my believing and am often brought back to the love that beats at the center of things by being close to the draft and the dying. The helplessness and vulnerability of people touches me deeply and reveals to me not only my own daftness and dying but God's too. God's daftness and dying are for my sake. What I wonder at is that this awesome vulnerability becomes an instrument of transfiguration. Hatred is transfigured into love, cursing into joy, the greatest weakness into the resilient energy of a caring passion.

The Church celebrates the fiery contradiction of dying and rising in the Feast of the Transfiguration (August 6). It is a feast of light. It honors the time when Peter, James, and John saw Christ, transfigured on the mount, in the fullness of who he really was. He shone in anticipation of radiance of the Resurrection. Ahead of him was the Passion and the Crucifixion, but there, on the mount, the fullness and the joy of the end was radiantly present.

There is also another moment of brilliance that we commemorate. On August 5, 1945, the atomic bomb was dropped on Hiroshima. It was, by all accounts, a complete success. The message that reached the president on August 6 on board the *Augusta* read, "RESULTS CLEAR-CUT SUCCESSFUL IN ALL RESPECTS. VISIBLE EFFECTS GREATER THAN ANY TEST." There was tremendous cheering and excitement at what the president called "the greatest thing in history." Even after this devastating demonstration of killing brilliance, Japan was not ready to surrender and three days later another bomb lit up the skies and destroyed Nagasaki.

The dropping of the bombs was, of course, for the best of motives. The argument for launching the bombers on their mission was, in the end, to save lives. As President Truman said twenty years later, "I could not worry about what history would say about my personal morality. I made the only decision I ever knew how to make. I did what I thought was right."[2] How often doing what we thought was right does harm to others.

It is ironic that the first testing of the atomic bomb, only three weeks earlier at Los Alamos, had the code name "Trinity." The Trinity is a way of talking about God as Love: Trinity—the gift and sign of our unity and solidarity with one another; Trinity—the ball of fire and the mushroom cloud. That first testing became a gruesome parody of the sign that God continually dwells with God's people as they move through the wilderness of pilgrimage: the pillar of fire by night and the pillar of cloud by day. The doctrine of the Trinity, which expresses the continued vulnerability and availability of God, became a code word for a naked and insidious energy, the effects of which are felt by the survivors for generations. Los Alamos is worth a visit. The museum there is organized in such a way that one doesn't even have to think about the dangers of our using nuclear energy. The museum is a tribute to the gods of technology and amnesia: "We can do anything. We remember nothing."

The Feast of the Transfiguration, like all feasts of the Church, teaches something about ourselves by forcing us to think about two different kinds of burnings, two kinds of fire: the fire of God's love and the fire of human pride. Yet it is all one fire. The flame has two effects: one of radiance, the other of radiation. There is the promise of radiance in our transfiguration into the likeness of God. Radiance shines in us insofar as we are willing to be transformed into experiments in vulnerability. There is also the threat of our destruction by the searing radiation from a nuclear holocaust. T. S. Eliot, in his *Four Quartets*, brings both kinds of fire together:

> *The dove descending breaks the air*
> *With flame of incandescent terror*
> *Of which the tongues declare*
> *The one discharge from sin and error.*
> *The only hope, or else despair*
>   *Lies in the choice of pyre or pyre—*
>   *To be redeemed from fire by fire.*
> *Who then devised the torment? Love.*
> *Love is the unfamiliar Name*
> *Behind the hands that wove*
> *The intolerable shirt of flame,*
> *Which human power cannot remove.*

We only live, only suspire
Consumed by either fire or fire.[3]

Our destiny is to be burned by one fire or another and so be either transfigured or consumed. Our pilgrimage is the drama of this choice.

We suffer inwardly, because two loves vie for our attention: God's and a crippling self-love that is insatiable. I am not talking about the proper self-love that is the foundation of all healthy loving. I am, rather, referring to the kind of "love" that is not love at all but a compensation for not having a strong and true sense of *self*. There is a kind of devouring emptiness that masquerades as a self, and it is that which will destroy us. There's no way out of getting burned. "We only live, only suspire, consumed by either fire or fire." Which is it to be? The fire of God's love or the fire of perdition, of being "lost," of being cut off from the source of life? The author of the Letter to the Hebrews wrote:

> *Remember where you stand: not before the palpable, blazing fire of Sinai, with darkness, gloom, and whirlwind... The kingdom we are given is unshakable; let us, therefore give thanks to God, and so worship him as he would be worshipped, with reverence and awe; for our God is a devouring fire.* (Heb. 12:18ff, NEB)

There is no escape from fire; but we do have a dramatic choice between God's flames and those of our own making. The alternative to God's fire is our own burnout—personally and globally.

Part of the world's threatened "burnout" has to do with the collapse of religion into a device for sanctioning our own private desires and the tyrannical view of "science" that claims too much for itself. Religion easily degenerates into sentimentalism or fanaticism, and the popular view of science is little more than a way of our worshiping an approach to technology understood as a mighty instrument of ego gratification. The ego, however, will never be satisfied, except in surrender. The fear of surrender is the peculiar form its suffering takes. Neither religion nor science is much help against the fires that face us.

The philosopher William James looked for a way of living "intellectually and emotionally in a universe that the collapse of traditional religion and the tyranny of science have laid waste."[4] Those two phrases are important: *the collapse of religion and the tyranny of science.* James deplored the terrible restriction of our horizon by our theoretical preconceptions, by our rush into easy and superficial understandings of things. If our horizons are to be expanded, we need to repress our desire to interpret reality prematurely. Our world is full of entrepreneurs packaging reality for the consumer. Those with the most money and power imagine that they can determine what is real for the rest of the world. They become the interpreters. But we know that the driven imagination of a revolutionary can also define reality. We are hungry for clear definitions, however false and misleading. People want to be told who they are and to know what's what.

William James not only identified the true source of the religious impulse but also the tyranny of the old science dogma of mechanistic materialism. This is the point of view (for example) that rightly angers and terrifies those who advocate "creation science" as over against evolution. Their conclusions are absurd, but I respect their instincts. The creationists reject a scientific humanism that would deny the fire of free will. So do I. The myth of nineteenth-century "science" is very much alive and is still taken for granted today "by thousands of scientists, journalists, and their docile listeners."[5] In fact, the reductionist tendencies of the so-called scientific point of view nearly drove the young William James crazy. He clung to two convictions: "the thought of my having a will and of my belonging to the brotherhood of men."[6] We might translate those convictions into a form for today as the need for a sense of purpose beyond ourselves and for an appreciation of the solidarity of the human race. These are the two fiery truths our pilgrimage continually teaches us.

We are not very good at choosing goals that do justice to the mystery of human reality. Still less are we skilled at giving life our focused attention. We choose goals that disappoint and diminish us as human beings. The choosing of a worthy goal is a matter of faith. Attending to it is a matter of prayer. From the Christian point of view a proper choice of the goal and the commitment to attend to it inevitably involves choosing and being committed to others, all the others—the human family. Bombing them soon ceases to be an option, as do all forms of oppression and injustice. In short, what we choose to do makes a difference, because in our choices we enter the flames of either love or damnation. When we choose love, we naturally choose each other. We belong to one another. In the end there is no "them." There is only "us." We are made one in the crucible of love.

James reached in part to what creationists rightly fear today. Julian Huxley and other late-nineteenth-century scientists had come up with a view of human beings as automata. The so-called scientific view was that we have no free will and are, therefore, incapable of faith and commitment. Today there is still a misplaced confidence in our rationality. James sought an antidote to reductionism and despair. The hard thing for us, who take for granted the scientific method, is to learn that "analysis and reduction distort." It is very useful to reduce things to their individual components, but it is vital to have a vision or overview of the whole at the same time. We suffer from an overvaluing of our rational powers. When we do that, we tend to give too much weight to the voice of the cynic inside us. There is often a progression from self-contempt to contempt for others. The fire within us begins to work against us. It is at this point that we are tempted to drop the bombs.

We may seem to have wandered a long way from Hiroshima and Nagasaki. But we haven't. The danger of a nuclear holocaust is rendered all the more possible by those who do not believe the two cardinal doctrines concerning human transfiguration: the freedom of the will and the solidarity of humankind. These feed the fire that keeps us alive. There are even militaristic religious people who hope for a literal nuclear Armageddon, in order to hasten the coming of the Reign of God! Their apocalyptic ravings become part of a political plan. Underneath is a contempt for those who don't "believe" or don't belong. Such an attitude relies on the assumption that millions of people simply don't count. The fires reserved for them are the fires of damnation. Only the chosen few matter—whether that chosen few be an elitist sect, a race that sees itself superior, or a group of scientists who are "in the know." The fire of such elitism is raging even now and cutting us off from one another. But there is, thank God, another fire, more powerful, that burns (sometimes quietly, sometimes explosively) in the hearts of men and women. It is the fire of Transfiguration, the fire of God's love.

Our burning and our transfiguration can be seen in the kind of human behavior depicted in the Bible. In Exodus (16:2–15) we read of the Israelites complaining in the wilderness and longing for the fleshpots of Egypt. The Israelites went in for a slow burn. They *murmured*. And God provided quails, and the Israelites made themselves sick! God also sent them bread from heaven, manna in the wilderness. They persistently missed the point that it was God who looked after them and loved them. They suffered from hardness of heart. What burned up the Israelites is what burns us up. We are consumed by our consumerism. We think we are possessing and devouring things, and it is they that are enslaving and consuming us. There's a bewildered look we sometimes see, out of the corner of our eye, on each other's faces—as if to say, "With all that I have, I *should* be happy. Why aren't I?" That look in our eye and in the eyes of others is the sign of the fire inside pushing us into pilgrimage.

We need a new way of looking at things. The writer of the Epistle to the Ephesians (4:17–25) knew that hardness of heart destroyed people's souls. They had hearts of stone. How terrible to be transfigured by greed and callousness into stone. The spiritual truth behind all this is that we become what we love. If we look lovingly at anything for long enough, we take on its characteristics. It is said that our faces are maps of our living and our loving. I think there is something in this. People *do* seem to look like their pets, and (more seriously) those who have loved each other for a long time begin to look like each other.

We have to take care what we love, because our loving determines our living. The gospel promises us a new mind and a new heart—a heart of flesh. "You must be made new in mind and spirit, and put on the new nature of God's creating, which shows itself in the just and devout life called for by the truth" (Eph. 4:23–24, NEB). Our destiny lies in the fire of God's love. Yet the mystery of human freedom is such that we can choose to go against the very grain of our own nature. We can turn the fire against us. We can destroy ourselves. We can diminish ourselves and others. We can go to hell. The mystery of the fire at the heart of things is this: people are not sent to hell. They go there.

Hell and its fires are metaphors for our missing the point of our lives by refusing to go on pilgrimage. In the Gospel (John 6:24–35) Jesus tries to get the people to see the point. They had seen Jesus feed the multitude. They remembered that God provided manna in the wilderness. But they were more concerned with the signs that Jesus performed than with who he was. Their attention was on their desire for security (bread) and not on the One who is our hope (the bread of God). Jesus says, "I am the bread of life; he who comes to me shall not hunger, and he who believes in me shall never thirst." Not to discern the true bread is to be consumed by a useless passion for bread that leaves an aching void inside us. Can we tell the true bread from the false? One nourishes us. The other leaves us ravenous. Which bread will we choose? Which will we choose as a nation, as a world community?

If we dare take a look at our grandiose expectations about American power, and if we are willing to embrace a more modest definition of our "interests," chances of a one great Burnout are diminished. It is not accidental that an unrealistic foreign policy leads to domestic disillusionment. We are ripe, at this point in our history, for scapegoating, witchhunts, and book burning. Something has to burn. And one of these things that we have to burn is our illusion that for us in the West all things are possible. You can't be sure of your vacation abroad because it just might be your flight that's hijacked. No airport is safe from terrorists. There is nowhere that is safe. Solutions have to be found in communion with others or not at all.

I long for our transfiguration. I pray that we may not only exercise our freedom but know that we are indeed free to exercise it. Pilgrims of the Spirit are those who choose the radiance of God's love rather than the radiation of self-interest. The pain and the fire are in the broken bread and the cup of wine of the Wedding Banquet. If we can live into the truth that the world is a wedding and that everyone is invited, we may be able to ensure that Hiroshima and Nagasaki will remain the signs of a "Never Again" rather than of a "One Day Soon." The fire that we need is very close to us. The God of Passion, the God of Fire says, "Come and eat. Come and drink. Come and be radiant." The pilgrimage comes to an end in the fire of God's passionate love for us. We are brought to

a condition of complete simplicity
(Costing not less than everything)
And all shall be well and
All manner of thing shall be well
When the tongues of flame are in-folded
Into the crowned knot of fire
And the fire and the rose are one.[7]

Our broken bones are knit together in the fire of God's love. The poet Dante envisioned heaven as a great white rose. We come home to a "crowned knot of fire" that is the result of the collision of the two great passions we have been exploring: our passion for God and God's Passion for us. Our homecoming is like finding ourselves part of a great white rose, the purpose of which is to be radiant with love.

STUDY QUESTIONS

1. Jones has invited us on a journey, looking at the cycle of the Church Year as "an opportunity to deepen our wildest longings." We have looked at our brokenness and vulnerability and even at

our hatred of and disagreement with God. "At the end we are to take each other to our hearts" (p. 181). What has been helpful in this study in guiding your walk between active participation in creating a human community and grateful acceptance of the freely offered love of God? What images from Jones's writings echo most clearly in your consciousness? Why?

2. Jones names the contrast between the Holy Trinity and the "Trinity" testing of the atomic bomb as well as the contrast between the radiance of God's love and the radiation of our own crippling self-love. He uses these to illustrate that we have a dramatic choice in life between seeking to follow God and seeking to follow our own insatiable egos. How often are you conscious of this choice? What guides your decision making and helps you evaluate your choice? How is it for you to stand before this choice?

3. "We suffer from an overvaluing of our rational powers," Jones insists. "…We tend to give too much weight to the voice of the cynic inside us" (p. 186). What guidelines or safety measures might be used to guard against overvaluing our rational powers? Where is it appropriate to rely solidly on such thinking?

4. In his introduction, Jones suggested three simple commitments required by the change of heart that is repentance: rigorous honesty, honoring of our passion for connection, and the search for a common language (pp. 5–6). How do these help us to see that "the fire that we need is very close to us"? In what ways do they help us to come home and fulfill our purpose, "to be radiant with love"?

5. With your deepened understanding of the pilgrimage of the seasons of Lent, Holy Week, and Easter, would you choose again to embark on such a journey? What resources will you need to continue choosing God? Where will you seek them?

NOTES

Introduction: Broken Bones May Joy!

1. Allan Bloom, *The Closing of the American Mind* (New York: Simon and Schuster, 1987), 381.
2. Alan Webster, *Broken Bones May Joy* (London; S.C.M. Press, 1968).
3. Lewis Lapham, *Harper's,* November 1986, 8.
4. Robin Lovin, *Books and Religion*, April 1986, 5.
5. Carl Raschke, "Religious Studies and the Default of the Critical Intelligence," *Journal of the American Academy of Religion* (Spring 1986): 135.
6. Raschke, "Religious Studies," 132.
7. Alasdair MacIntyre, *After Virtue: A Study in Moral Theory* (Notre Dame, IN: Univ. of Notre Dame Press, 1981), 245, and quoted by David Hollenbach, S.J., "Justice as Participation: Public Moral Discourse and the U.S. Economy," (1986): 5.
8. Hollenbach, "Justice as Participation," 21.

1. The Same Old Story

1. Allan Bloom, *The Closing of the American Mind* (New York: Simon and Schuster, 1987), 67.
2. Milan Kundera, *The Unbearable Lightness of Being* (New York: Harper & Row, 1984), 5.
3. See Oliver Sacks, *The Man Who Mistook His Wife for a Hat* (New York, Harper & Row, 1986).
4. Mary Durack, *The Rock and the Sand* (London, Gorgi Books, 1985), 21.
5. Milan Kundera, *The Book of Laughter and Forgetting* (New York: Penguin, 1980).

2. The Road That Leads Nowhere

1. Allan Bloom, *The Closing of the American Mind* (New York: Simon & Schuster, 1987), 228.
2. Suzanne Britt, *Books and Religion*, January 1987.
3. John Climacus, *The Ladder of Divine Ascent*, trans. Colm Luibheid and Norman Russell (New York, Paulist Press, 1982), 121.
4. John Updike, *Roger's Version* (New York: Knopf, 1986), 273.
5. *New York Times*, March 15, 1987.
6. Augustine, *Confessions*, trans. R. S. Pine-Coffin (Harmondsworth: Penguin, 1961), 177–78.

7. Ibid., 231. See the translation of this passage in *The Lord of the Journey*, ed. Roger Pooley and Philip Seddon (London: Collins, 1986), 73.

8. Richard Baxter, *The Autobiography*, quoted by Pooley and Seddon, *The Lord of the Journey*, 80.

9. See Jeffrey Burton Russell, "The Devin in a Warring World," *Books and Religion*, January 1987.

10. John Bunyon, *Pilgrim's Progress*, ed. J. B. Wharey, rev. Roger Sharrock (Oxford: Clarendon Press, 1960), 38.

3. Home—The Last Place on Earth

1. Paul Tournier, *The Adventure of Living* (London: S.C.M. Press, 1966), 38–39.

2. Abraham Joshua Heschel, *The Insecurity of Freedom* (New York: Schocken Books, 1966) 3. See also John C. Merkle, *The Genesis of Faith: The Depth Theology of Abraham Joshua Heschel* (New York: Macmillan, 1985), 28ff.

3. Abraham Joshua Heschel, *God in Search of Man: A Philosophy of Judaism* (New York: Farrar, Straus, and Cudahy, 1955), 140–41.

4. See St. Gregory's *Life of Moses* (New York: Paulist Press).

5. Allan Bloom, *The Closing of the American Mind* (New York: Simon and Schuster, 1987), 134–35.

6. See Robert Hughes, *The Fatal Shore* (New York: Knopf, 1987).

7. Iris Murdoch, *The Good Apprentice* (New York: Viking Press, 1986), 44.

8. Ibid.

9. Graham Greene, *A Burnt-Out Case* (New York: Viking Press, 1961), 57.

10. Ibid.

11. Ibid., 189–98.

4. The Search for Light

1. Iris Murdoch, *The Nice and the Good* (New York: Viking Press, 1968), 308–29. See also my book *Soul Making* (San Francisco: Harper & Row, 1985), chapter 3.

2. Quoted by Kate Millett in *Flying* (New York: Ballantine, 1974), 445.

3. Ruth Tiffany Barnhouse, *Clergy and the Sexual Revolution* (Washington DC: Alban Institute, 1987), 49.

4. Robert Bellah, ed., *Uncivil Religion* (New York: Crossroads, 1987), 229.

5. Ibid., 230–31.

6. Allan Bloom, *The Closing of the American Mind* (New York: Simon and Schuster, 1987), 27.

7. See *New York Review of Books*, April 9, 1987, 18.

8. Ibid.

9. Ibid.

5. A Heart Willing to Give Itself Away

1. Keri Hulme, *The Bone People* (London: Pan Books [Picador], 1986), 4.
2. C. D. Bartholomew, *The God of Chance* (London: S.C.M. Press, 1984), 187.
3. This owes a great deal to the writings of Karl Rahner.

6. God Has Fallen in Love with You and Wants You to Come Home

1. Walker Percy, *The Thanatos Syndrome* (New York: Farrar, Straus, and Giroux, 1987), 88.

7. Homecoming—Facing What We Dread

1. Jacques Barzun, *A Stroll with William James* (New York: Harper & Row, 1983), 17.
2. Quoted by Barzun, *A Stroll with William James*, 17.
3. Harry Williams, *The True Wilderness* (London: Pelican, 1965), 29.
4. W. H. Auden, *Collected Longer Poems* (New York: Vintage, 1975), 163.
5. James Hillman, *Inter Views* (New York: Harper & Row, 1984).
6. Ibid., 126–29.
7. Ibid.
8. André Louf, *Cistercian Studies 2* (1975): 131.
9. William Golding, *Darkness Visible* (New York, Farrar, Straus and Giroux, 1979), 193.
10. Ibid., 200.
11. Alice Walker, *The Color Purple* (New York: Harcourt Brace Jovanovich, 1982), 167.

8. Home Means Freedom to Become a Family

1. See also Michael Davie and Simon Davie, eds., *The Faber Book of Cricket* (London: Faber, 1987).
2. W. B. Yeats, "Supernatural Songs V," in *The Poems of W. B. Yeats* (New York: Macmillan, 1983), 286. "Ribh Considers Christian Love is insufficient."
3. Fyodor Dostoyevski, *The Brothers Karamazov*, trans. Constance Garnett (New York: Random House, Modern Library, 1912), 251–54.
4. Ibid., 255–74.

9. Come Home! All Is Forgiven!

1. John C. Merkle, *The Genesis of Faith: The Depth Theology of Abraham Joshua Heschel* (New York: Macmillan, 1985), 72.

2. See Patrick Henry, "On Teaching Christianity: How to Make the Familiar Surprising," *The Council on the Study of Religion Bulletin* (February 1985): 1ff.

3. See Virginia Owens, *The Total Image* (Grand Rapids, MI: Eerdmans, 1983).

4. *The Book of Common Prayer*, 1979, 865.

5. John Updike, *The Witches of Eastwick* (New York: Knopf, 1985).

6. James Hillman, *Inter Views* (New York: Harper & Row, 1984), 11.

7. Ibid., 130–31.

8. Ibid., 141.

9. See Linda Blandford, *Manchester Guardian Weekly*, February 17, 1985, 19.

10. Ibid., 126–29.

11. Hillman *Inter Views*.

12. W. H. Auden, *Twelve Songs*, XII.

11. The Tree Joining Heaven and Earth

1. Amy Carmichael in *The Lord of the Journey*, eds. Roger Pooley and Philip Seddon (London: Collins, 1986), 333.

2. Marcos Ana, trans. Chloe Valliamy and Stephen Sodley, in *Short Prayers for the Long Day*, comp. Giles Harcourt and Melville Harcourt (London: Collins, 1978), 77.

3. Frederick Buechner, *Brendan*, (New York: Atheneum, 1987), 166.

4. Ibid., 126.

5. Helen Waddell, *Peter Abelard*, 200–201.

12. Easter Is Now!

1. Quoted by John C. Merkle, *The Genesis of Faith* (New York: Macmillan, 1985), 153.

2. Ibid., 156.

3. Ibid.

4. H. G. Baynes, *Analytical Psychology and the English Mind* (London: Methuen, 1950), 69.

5. Marie-Louise von Franz, *The Problem of Puer Aeternus* (Zurich: Spring Publications, 1970), 1–2.

6. John Cheever, "John Cheever: The Art of Fiction LXII," *Paris Review* 17 (Fall 1976): 64.

7. "John Hersey Talks with John Cheever," *Yale Alumni Magazine and Journal*, December 1977, 24.

13. Easter—The Hope of Glory

1. From "Shadows," in *D. H. Lawrence—The Complete Poems*, ed. Vivian De Sola Pinto and F. Warren Roberts (London: Penguin Books, 1977).

2. Walker Percy, *The Thanatos Syndrome* (New York: Farrar, Straus and Giroux, 1987).

14. The Drama in Our Bones

1. Anthony de Mello, *The Song of the Bird* (New York: Doubleday, 1984), 115–16.
2. Quoted by George Steiner in *George Steiner: A Reader* (London: Penguin Books, 1984), 36.
3. Frederick Buechner, *Brendan* (New York: Atheneum, 1987), 211–12.
4. Anne Sexton, *The Awful Rowing Toward God* (Boston: Houghton Mifflin, 1975), 61.

15. The Fire of Love

1. Frederick Buechner, *Brendan* (New York: Atheneum, 1987), 237.
2. Margaret Truman, *Harry S. Truman* (New York: William Morrow, 1973), 567.
3. T. S. Eliot, "Little Gidding," section 5 in *The Four Quartets* (London: Folio Society, 1967).
4. Jacques Barzun, *A Stroll with William James* (New York, Harper & Row, 1983), 16–17.
5. Ibid., 16.
6. Ibid.
7. T. S. Eliot, "Little Gidding," section 5 in *The Four Quartets* (London, Folio Society, 1967).

SELECT BIBLIOGRAPHY

Auden, W. H. *Selected Poetry*. New York: Vintage, 1978.

Augustine. *The Confessions*. London: Penguin.

Donne, John. *Devotions on Emergent Occasions*. Atlantic Highlands, NJ: Humanities, 1975.

Eliot, T. S. "The Cocktail Party" in *The Complete Poems and Plays*. New York: Harcourt, Brace & Jovanovich, 1962.

Golding, William. *Free Fall*. New York: Harcourt, Brace & Jovanovich, 1962.

Julian of Norwich. *Revelations of Divine Love*. London: Penguin.

Percy, Walker. *The Movie-Goer*. New York: Avon, 1960.

Purtill, Richard. *C. S. Lewis's Case for the Christian Faith*. San Francisco: Harper & Row, 1981.

Studdert, Kennedy. *TheWicket Gate*. New York: Doubleday, 1929.